MY MOST MEMORABLE ADVENTURES
ONE HUNTING AND ONE FISHING

COPYRIGHT (C) BY BILL R. THOMAS

ALL RIGHTS RESERVED

PRINTED IN THE UNITED STATES OF AMERICA

HUNTING STORY

TO DON JOSE ANTONIO NIETO*

AND

TO MY MEXICAN HUNTING GUIDES AND COMPADRES
JUAN & MARCELLO*

FISHING STORY

TO MY ALASKAN FISHING BUDDIES
DEWEY*, ROY*, TOM, EDDIE*, DON, WALLACE*, & JOHN

AND THE ENTIRE STAFF AT LAKE CLARK LODGE

BUT MOST OF ALL, THIS BOOK WAS WRITTEN AS A TRIBUTE
TO MY FATHER-IN-LAW, DON JOSE ANTONIO NIETO (DECEASED),
MUY GRANDE HOMBRE

*DECEASED

INTRODUCTION

I'VE BEEN HUNTING AND FISHING FOR AS LONG AS I CAN REMEMBER. I CUT MY TEETH ON A .22 RIFLE BARREL AND WAS BRINGING MEAT TO THE TABLE BY THE TIME I WAS TEN. ALSO, I WHILED AWAY MANY MEMORABLE HOURS ON THE CREEK BANK WITH A CANE POLE ,TIGHT LINE AND A WORM ON THE HOOK. THERE IS NO JOY LIKE GOD'S GREAT OUTDOORS.

IN THE FIRST ADVENTURE I'LL TAKE YOU ON A "MIXED BAG" HUNTING TRIP THROUGH THE SIERRA MADRE MOUNTAINS OF MEXICO WITH MY TWO MEXICAN GUIDES AND FRIENDS, JUAN AND MARCELLO.

IN THE NEXT STORY WE'LL SPEND A COUPLE OF WEEKS IN SOUTH CENTRAL ALASKA – HOPPING (VIA CESSNA WITH FLOATS) FROM ONE EXTRAORDINARY FISHING HOLE TO ANOTHER EVEN BETTER.

THESE TWO ADVENTURES ARE THE MOST MEMORABLE OF MY LONG CAREER AS A HUNTER AND FISHERMAN.

I HOPE YOU ENJOY RELIVING THEM WITH ME. THANKS.

BILL THOMAS

MY MOST MEMORABLE ADVENTURES
ONE HUNTING AND ONE FISHING

CONTENTS

CHAPTER		PAGE
MIXED BAG IN THE SIERRA MADRES (HUNTING)		1
1.	DELAY EN ROUTE (CHRISTMAS 1956) AND THE TRIP TO THE EL TREBOL RANCH (ADVENTURE ITSELF)	2
2.	PLANNING THE HUNT-DUMB GRINGO	9
3.	TRAPPING THE PERNICE AND THE FIRST NIGHT IN CAMP	15
4.	VENADO!	19
5.	EL GATO	23
6.	SURROUNDED BY JAVELINA	27
7.	IT LOOKED LIKE PANCHO VILLA…HIMSELF	33
8.	INDIAN VILLAGE	39
9.	MAS VENADOS	43
10.	THE TRIP HOME	54

MY MOST MEMORABLE ADVENTURES
ONE HUNTING AND ONE FISHING

CONTENTS - Continued

CHAPTER		PAGE
ALASKAN SMORGASBOARD (FISHING)		1
1.	PLANNING THE TRIP	2
2.	NORTH – TO ALASKA	10
3.	ANCHORAGE, ALASKA	16
4.	LAKE ILIAMNA	19
5.	LAKE CLARK LODGE	23
6.	KINGS ON THE MULCHATNA	33
7.	THE AMERICAN RIVER - CHAR & TROUT	51
8.	SOCKEYES AT LAKE ILIAMNA	64
9.	FLOATING THE TAZIMINA	72
10.	NORTHERN PIKE	80
11.	LAKE TROUT ON LAKE CLARK	87

MIXED BAG IN THE SIERRA MADRES (HUNTING)

CHAPTER 1

DELAY EN ROUTE (CHRISTMAS 1956) AND THE TRIP TO THE EL TREBOL (ADVENTURE IN ITSELF)

Caro and I had been married for less than six months. I was on active duty in the Air Force and had just completed navigation training at Waco, Texas and my next assignment was bombardier training in Sacramento, California. It was almost Christmas and I was given a two week delay en route. Things were working out nicely for us to spend Christmas with her parents in Presidio, Texas - almost the mid point in our trip to California. Presidio is on the border with Mexico - just west of where the Rio Grande makes a "Big Bend". We packed up our possessions (clothing & TV set) and loaded them into our new Chevrolet Bel Air and said goodbye to Waco. There was snow and ice on the highway in West Texas and it took all day to drive to Presidio - we arrived after dark.

Presidio is a quiet little town. Ojinaga, Mexico sits on the other side of the Rio Grande. After two days of visiting, shopping, and sightseeing I was starting to get bored. I had seen all there was to see from front to back and side to side and I had bought all I intended to buy. Don Jose, my new father in law, detected my boredom and asked if I enjoyed ranching, horseback riding, and hunting? My response was

"Does a one legged duck swim in a circle?" - or something equally brilliant. None the less, when he saw how I perked up at the mention of hunting he invited me to join him the next morning for a trip to his ranch down in Mexico. He said we would be gone at least a week -maybe longer- but would be back by Christmas Eve. It took some convincing by me and Jose but Caro finally gave me permission to go.

I immediately started unpacking things from our car which I felt I would need on the trip -blue jeans, wool shirts, coat, cowboy boots & hat, camera, rifle, hunting knife, etc. When Caro saw the pile of gear I had stacked she suddenly realized I was going to be gone for several days and she began to get angry. (she had accepted several invitations to parties, dances, fiestas, etc.) I had to make some rash promises to settle her down and keep peace in the family. I went to the general store (her uncle's) and purchased ammo, film, cigarettes, gum, etc. and was set to go. The only guns I owned at the time were a Winchester carbine (thirty-thirty or trinta-trinta as they say in Espanol) and a Remington bolt action .22(biente dos). I decided to take both guns since I had no idea what I would be hunting. My father in law was not much help since he did not hunt. He thought there were deer, bear, lions, javelinas, jackrabbits, quail, and no telling what else where I would be hunting.

The next morning we had an early breakfast and started loading his GMC pickup for the trip to the ranch. Jose took inventory of my gear and picked up my guns, camera, ammo, and knife and wrapped them in a blanket and placed them in the bed of the pickup. Only my clothes and personal effects remained in my B4 bag which was loaded in the cab. We said goodbye to the ladies and drove to his brother's general store. There we loaded salt and mineral blocks, cattle vaccine, 100 # bags of pinto beans, bags of salt and sugar, Christmas gifts, nuts and candy, some hardware stuff, etc. in the pickup bed. We next covered everything in the bed with a large tarp and then covered the tarp with several bales of hay. Lastly, he stacked a couple of cases of canned peaches on top of the hay. Jose threw a couple of cartons of cigarettes and a big sack of hard candy in the cab, handed me a wad of pesos , and we climbed aboard and were on our way. I was mighty curious as to why he had packed as he did but didn't ask any questions and he didn't volunteer any explanation. I figured he knew what he was doing.

We stopped at the Border Patrol station on this side of the Rio Grande (no problems) they all knew Don Jose as he went to his ranch every month with a similarly loaded truck. We crossed the bridge and stopped at the Mexican station. One of the guards started to examine the trucks. He was on my side so Jose whispered “Give him a pack of cigarettes and twenty pesos.” I did as he instructed and the guard smiled and said

“Pasar” and went back inside. We drove away and next stopped at a bakery in Ojinaga and bought pan (bread) and pan dulce (sweet bread), then stopped at a saddle shop and picked up a saddle that had been left for repair, and our last stop was at a service station where we fueled the truck for the long trip to the ranch. We also filled two spare 5 gallon tanks with gasoline and another with diesel fuel.

Then we headed south and in about ten blocks the pavement ended and we were on a dirt road. It was rough and bumpy. Jose told me to get used to it – we had over 100 miles of bumpy dirt road ahead before reaching his ranch. I commented “Sure hope it doesn’t rain” and Jose responded “Me too.”

We continued southward on the dirt road, averaging less than 20 miles per hour. There were no bridges and we forded a couple of shallow streams. When we crossed the second one, water splashed up on the distributor and the truck quit running. We sat in the middle of the creek for maybe an hour until it dried out and the truck restarted. It was a very remote and arid region (northern Chihuahua). While we sat there, several deer came to the creek to drink and I got excited and wanted to unpack my rifle and shoot at them. Jose said "No, we’re too close to a check point".

After the truck restarted and we had gone about a mile, we came upon three adobe huts-literally out in the middle of nowhere. As we approached them about a dozen uniformed Mexican soldiers poured out of the huts and lined up across thc dirt road. Jose stopped the truck and we got out as El Jefe approached. Jose spoke to him in Spanish and they embraced. Then Jose introduced me and after El Jefe looked me over from top to bottom he said "Mucho gusto Guillermo" and gave me a bear hug. I liked him immediately. Jose gave him a carton of cigarettes and yelled something to the troops in Spanish and they came to the truck and lined up. Jose took a case of peaches and handed each soldier a can of peaches as they passed by. I figured out the drill and got the sack of candy and handed each of them some candy. Jose and El Jefe went inside the office and in a couple of minutes Jose returned and we got into the truck and were on our way. I finally said "Now I understand why we brought the peaches, candy, and cigarettes". He laughed and explained that he had been doing the same thing for twenty five years. He said the soldiers were young and very lonely out on the Fronteria and since there were no towns or stores for miles-money meant nothing to them. However they all had a sweet tooth and he learned that canned peaches were the best "gift" you could use to clear the interior check point. He further explained that he and the chief were old friends and he always brought him U.S. cigarettes and a few pesos and would bring him some beef on the return trip.

We continued bumping and bouncing down the road and in about two hours came into the small village of LaMula. The fields around the village had been tilled and rows of dried corn stalks covered most of them. Jose explained that the people living here were agrarians who had "squatted" on this land after the revolution and the original owners had been killed during the revolution. He feared that someday they would also try to steal his ranch. There were about 20 adobe huts in this village-they lined both sides of the road. When we reached the center of them, Jose stopped the truck and started blowing the horn. As heads appeared in the doorways Jose rolled down the window and yelled "Feliz Navidad". All the villagers converged on the truck and we found ourselves surrounded. Jose instructed me to pass out candy to the children and he began passing out canned peaches to the adults. To these poor people, Don Jose was Santa Clause himself. It was a touching experience. My respect for my new father in law increased dramatically- as it would continue to so do throughout this trip.

After two or three more hours of bouncing down the dusty, bumpy road we finally turned off on a side road and went under a huge arc over cattle guards. A sign hung from the arch-El Trebol (also the emblem of a four leaf lover). Jose proudly announced "we are home." You could tell how proud of the ranch he was and rightly so. We drove for at least another fifteen minutes before the ranch headquarters came into view. There were fat Herford cows and calves everywhere you looked. The ranch headquarters looked like an army fort from old western movie. A stone fence about six feet tall surrounded about an acre of land. A two story stucco building stood up in one corner and a water tower stood up in the center-it was painted red and had El Trebol (four leaf clover) painted on it in large white letters along with the cloverleaf emblem(which was his cattle brand). I opened the gate and we drove inside.

There were four adobe houses inside the walls along with a water well (windmill powered), gardens, a large orchard, and many tropical trees - a veritable tropical paradise out in the middle of no man's land. Four families lived there and worked the ranch. There were little kids all over the place shouting "El Patron (owner, boss, chief). Jose parked the truck under the two story building. The ground floor contained the garage, storage room, and a shop. The second floor contained a bedroom, small kitchen, and a large den with a fireplace- El Patron's quarters. All four families converged upon us and Jose introduced me to everyone. After many "mucho gustos" (pleased to meet you) we began to unload the truck. Don Jose passed out Christmas presents while Marcello, one of the cowboys went to hitch up a team of horses to a wagon and returned in a few minutes to haul the hay, salt, mineral blocks, etc. to the barn which was located outside the walled compound. One of the older children carried firewood upstairs and built a fire. I unloaded my guns and gear and carried them upstairs. The beans, salt, sugar, etc. were unloaded and placed in the storeroom. It was a festive atmosphere and everyone was happy-they were talking 100 mph in Spanish and although I understood a word now and then- I really didn't know what the heck was going on.

CHAPTER 2

PLANNING THE HUNT - DUMB GRINGO

It was very late in the day and dusk was fast approaching and Jose asked if I would like to see a little of the ranch before supper. At the mention of supper I realized how hungry I was (we had not eaten since breakfast) and I replied "Sure, but before we go is there anything to eat- I'm starved". He said something in Spanish and one of the older boys left and one of the older girls ducked into the storeroom. She returned in a minute and handed me this dried stringy hemp rope looking stuff, smiled and said 'jerky". Jose instructed me to chew it like gum. I chomped down on it and started chewing- it got better with each chomp. By the time the young boy returned with two saddled horses, my hunger was gone. I got a drink of water and swung into the saddle on a bay mare. Jose was already mounted on a dun gelding. We rode through the gate and made a swing through the west pasture - stopping at a windmill to water the horses. We must have seen a thousand cows on this short swing. We also flushed several coveys of quail and jumped a few deer and some coyotes. By the time we returned to headquarters it was dark. We could see the glow of a fire inside the wall and hear music and singing, Don Jose said "Fiesta Time". One of the boys met us at the gate and took the horses. We went inside and washed up and joined the ranch families around the fire. One of the men was roasting chunks of beef on a spit over the fire and a big iron kettle of beans was simmering at the edge of the fire. A dutch oven full of tortillas and a huge blackened coffee pot sat at the edge of the coals. We got plates and silverware and loaded up on broiled beef, beans ,tortillas, and the hottest sauce this side of the equator. I was so hungry I ate everything. The children were impressed with my ability to handle the muy caliente jalapenos (very hot peppers). I got a cup of the strong coffee, lit a cigarette, found a chair and settled down to enjoy the music. The band consisted of one of the men with an old violin, another with a bass guitar, a young girl with an accordion, a young boy with a battered trumpet, and one of the women with a guitar. They really were quite good and their voices were excellent-even though I could not understand a word they were singing. When the band took a break to eat, Jose called two of the cowboys (Juan and Marcello) over and instructed them to take me hunting. They smiled ear to ear-both loved to hunt. We tried to converse with Jose acting as interpreter but were having some difficulty so I found a stick and started drawing in the dirt by the light of the fire as I tried to explain my thoughts. Soon we were surrounded by all the children who began giggling and laughing. Jose burst out laughing also and Juan and Marcello discretely joined the laughter. I asked "What is so funny?" "The children think you are dumb because you draw everything in the dirt and don't speak Spanish," Jose said. My response was "I am."

It was getting very late and I was getting sleepy-so was Jose. He told them, in effect, party's over, and we lit a Kerosene lantern and went upstairs to get ready for bed. Jose had a cot and blankets for me so I fixed my bed by the fireplace since it had gotten rather cold. Jose retired to his bedroom which contained a massive bed. I threw a couple of logs on the fire and crawled under the blankets on the cot. In seconds I was fast asleep it seemed that I had just gone to bed when I was awakened by a conversation in Spanish. I looked out the window and it was breaking day. A lantern was burning in the kitchen and I could smell coffee brewing and something cooking. I got up, dressed, went outside and found the outhouse and watered it down and came back inside and joined Jose, Juan, and Juan's wife (who was doing the cooking) in the kitchen. I got a cup of coffee and watched as she cooked a pan full of quail. When the birds were done she fried some eggs and heated some refried frijoles and tortillas. I can't remember a more delicious breakfast. Jose passed on my compliments to her and she smiled and said "de nada." (It was nothing.)

We had almost finished breakfast when Marcello joined us - he had already eaten and would only drink a cup of coffee with us. He said the horses were saddled and the pack horse was packed- he was ready to get moving. I finished eating and went to get my rifles, knife, ammo, and camera. Jose assured me that was all I needed to take- that Marcello had packed everything else. I grabbed three cartons of cigarettes too -just in case. As an afterthought, I also grabbed a couple of pair of underwear - you never know. While I was rummaging around gathering my gear, Jose was also rummaging around - obviously looking for something. He finally found them and had me sit in a chair while he strapped a pair of spurs on my boots. That was the first time in my life I had worn spurs and it took a couple of spills before I got used to them. They turned out to be very beneficial on the trip. I wore a heavy wool shirt, blue jeans, and put on a medium jacket and my new Stetson hat and announced I was ready to go. We went down to the tied horses and I put my stuff in the saddle bags on my horse and my Winchester in the scabbard. Marcello took my .22 and put it in his scabbard. Both Juan and Marcello were wearing six guns strapped around their waists. They didn't have rifles or shotguns. The ranch rifle was left at the ranch for protection. It was an old 7.65 mm Spanish mauser.

We climbed into the saddles and Juan led us through the gate and we headed west. Our general plan was to make a semi-circle through the Sierra Madre mountains to the west of El Trebol, which sat in the foothills to the east of the mountain range. We planned to travel west for three days before turning back to the east - that should put us back at ranch headquarters the night of the sixth day. The game we sought was basically "pot luck". The last thing that Jose gave me before we left was a note addressed to Sr. Wences Lau, his cousin who owned part of the land we would be hunting on.

In less than a mile from ranch headquarters, three deer jumped out of a small thicket and bounded off One of them had a small rack - looked like six points maybe. Instinctively I slid the Winchester from the saddle scabbard ,jacked a cartridge into the barrel, and took a hurried shot at the moving buck Simultaneous with the crack of the rifle , Juan yelled "No" and the bay mare I was riding started bucking. I was holding to the saddle horn and doing my best to stay on the bucking mare and caught a glimpse of Marcello on the ground with the .22 lined up for a shot In about three seconds the mare dislodged me and I went sailing through the air and landed hard on my butt. I still had the Winchester in my right hand. Both of the Mexican cowboys were laughing at me, the dumb gringo. I picked myself up and brushed off. Juan caught the mare and returned the mare to me and said something in Spanish as I climbed back into the saddle. I believe he said "Don't shoot from horseback again" and I didn't intend to.

Marcello had ridden off in the direction the deer had run so Juan and I followed him. By the time we caught up he had already dismounted and was in the process of field dressing a small doe. We dismounted and helped him. Marcello showed me where he had hit the deer - right below the ear. That was a running head shot of about 100 yards with a .22 rifle mind you - I was impressed. He finished skinning the deer and cut up the meat and wrapped it in the hide, said something in Spanish, and mounted his horse. Juan handed him the deer and he balanced it in front of his saddle and rode off. Juan made some sign language which I correctly interpreted to mean that Marcello was taking the meat back to the ranch and would catch up with us later. We mounted and continued on our westward journey. We jumped several coveys of quail and I wished that I had a shotgun - quail hunting is my favorite sport. Juan raised his hand and said "coyote" and pointed toward the south. I saw the coyote and slid the Winchester from the scabbard and dismounted. I took several steps away from the horse and Juan grabbed her bridle. He whistled and the coyote stopped and looked back at us. "Ka-Boom" the Winchester roared and the coyote dropped. Juan said "Bueno." I remounted and we rode over to take a look at it. Juan lifted the head and showed me the bullet hole. Luckily I had hit it right in the head. While we were examining the critter, Marcello rode up and Juan showed him the bullet hole and they talked in Spanish some and both looked at me and smiled. I think I had earned a little respect. They skinned the tail off the coyote and put it in a saddle bag. We took a break and smoked before mounting. I reached into the saddle bag on my horse and handed each of them a pack of Marlboro's. They thanked me and talked to one another in Spanish. I think they were complimenting me - don't know.

CHAPTER 3

TRAPPING PERNICE AND FIRST NIGHT IN CAMP

I tried to convey to them by sign language that a few pernice quail would be good for a meal. They said "Si" and we remounted and rode a couple of miles and stopped at a draw (a small shallow valley), and dismounted. They tied the horses to a mesquite tree and Marcello removed what appeared to be a conical shaped fish trap from his saddle bags and we all squatted and Juan got a stick and drew some pictures in the dirt and they tried to explain what we were about to do. One of the pictures appeared to be a bird and another was a large V with the fish trap (by sign language) being placed in the apex. It took a while but I finally figured out what we were up to - we were going to trap some pernice (quail). We dropped down in the valley and gathered brush and constructed a large V and Marcello got twigs to hold the net in place and placed it in the apex. Next we climbed back up on the ridge and circled to the mouth of the valley and dropped down off the ridge and formed a line across the valley and started walking toward the trap, yelling and throwing rocks into the cover as we walked.

Before we reached the trap I saw a covey of Mexican quail (which normally don’t fly unless hard pressed) on the ground ahead of us and they were heading toward the trap. Juan and Marcello had seen the quail also and were expertly herding them toward the open end of the V. Once they entered the V, Juan ran at them, making a shrill hawk like noise, and they scurried into the fish net Juan lifted the net and started removing quail and popping their heads off and dropping them on the ground. I followed Marcello's lead and started skinning quail and removing their entrails. Juan got a paper sack from the saddle bags and we put the dressed birds in it. We had 19 birds for a future feast.

About four o'clock in the afternoon we finally came to a fence - barbed wire strung on cedar posts. Juan dismounted and disconnected the two top wires from a post so we could jump the horses over and when we were across he reconnected the fence to the post. We were at the edge of the mountains and in minutes we were riding around the base of the nearest mountain and came to a canyon with a small stream flowing through it Juan rode ahead and called us when he located a good camp site. We rode into a small grassy clearing containing about two acres and dismounted. We unsaddled and unpacked the horses and started to set up our camp on the bank of the stream. Marcello took charge of the horses and watered them before he hobbled them in the lush *grass.* I gathered firewood as Juan started getting stuff ready to cook. Between the first and second loads of wood, Juan had built the fire and encircled it with large rocks. In minutes he had a large pot of coffee brewing. Marcello and I drank coffee and smoked and watched with some curiosity as Juan went down to the water and returned with two handfuls of mud. He next covered three quail, the deer heart, kidney, and liver with the mud and made mud balls of each and placed them in the coals. Finally he got a pan and poured about a quart of pre-cooked beans from a gallon jar and put the pan on the coals to warm and laid out some tortillas on a rock by the fire.

Juan poured himself a cup of coffee, lit a cigarette, and joined us. Now and then he would get a stick and move the mud balls around in the fire. He finally rolled them out of the coals and after they cooled he got three metal plates, cracked the mud balls, now rocks, and expertly removed the meat with a hunting knife and divided it on the plates, added a scoop of beans and a couple of tortillas to each plate, and passed them out. Marcello said something in Spanish and Juan answered "no" so Marcello went to his saddle bags and returned with a big grin on his face

and a quart jar of the fiery sauce in his hand. After he generously poured the hot stuff on his food he passed the sauce to me and I put a little bit of it on my meat and passed it to Juan who did likewise. We settled down to some serious eating and I was amazed at how delicious the meat turned out - especially the kidneys. It was a meal fit for a king. By the time we were finished eating it had grown dark and the stars had come out What a glorious night? We sat around the camp fire and sipped coffee ,smoked, and watched a shooting star streak across the heavens. I realized that we had spent an entire day without seeing another person or any signs of civilization. We were truly in the wilderness and I had an inkling of how the early pioneers must have felt and how Texas must have been a hundred years ago. We tried to carry on a conversation but finally gave up and went to bed. I was beginning to pick up a little (poco) Spanish, but darn little. I vowed to learn the language.

CHAPTER 4

VENADO!!!!

I am normally a light sleeper and an early riser. But this first night in camp was cold in the mountains and with a belly fill of meat and a warm bed by the fire, I slept like a baby and did not wake until daylight. I was awakened by Marcello who was shaking me and as soon as I opened

my eyes he whispered excitedly "Venado.......Venado Grande." He motioned for me to follow him. Juan was already busy with breakfast I flipped the blankets and tarp off me and slipped on my boots - didn't need to dress since I had slept in my clothes. I put on my coat and hat, grabbed the Winchester and a handful of shells, and followed Marcello. We went downstream a ways taking advantage of what little cover there was and he stopped and pointed out to the open field. The four horses were peacefully grazing and about 50 yards from them stood the largest buck that I had ever seen. It was a seven point (that's 7 on either side) mule deer and had to weigh well over 200 pounds. He was standing broadside so I aimed at his heart and touched off a round. I heard the bullet whack him and saw him stagger but he ran off anyway. I knew he was hit hard so I started to follow him. Marcello grabbed me by the arm and said "no" and more in Spanish that I could not understand so I stopped and followed him back to camp.

When we got back to camp, breakfast was ready. The bill of fare this morning was fried quail, warmed up beans, tortillas, and strong coffee - plus the red hot picante sauce of course. Juan and Marcello talked excitedly about the venado grande. As soon as we finished breakfast we walked to the spot where the deer had been standing when I shot. Juan said "muerta" and we found a small pool of blood which confirmed my hit. We started following the blood sign and in about 200 yards Juan said "Venado" and pointed. The big deer was laying in some brush up ahead - dead as a hammer. He was a magnificent animal - but what were we going to do with him? He was much too heavy to carry with us and it was a long way to the ranch. I made them understand that I wanted to keep the horns, but only the horns. They removed the horns, cut out chunks of the back strap, and removed the liver, heart, and kidneys and put them in a paper sack and in the saddle bags. It saddened me to leave all of that red meat but there was no other choice. I could tell it bothered them also. I decided then that I would not shoot any more deer until we got back close enough to ranch headquarters to pack the meat in.

As we were breaking camp Marcello was trying to tell me something about “El Gato Grande.” We finally got down to our pictures in the dirt and sign language. It took a while but I finally decided he wanted to know if I wanted to shoot a big cat – a mountain lion. I said "Si". He nodded and mounted his horse and rode off. In a little while he returned, dragging the deer carcass. I then understood fully – the big mule deer carcass was going to be big cat bait.

We spent all of this day winding our way deeper into the Sierra Madres. The going was rough even though we stuck to the canyons and went around the bases of the large mountains. Occasionally we were forced to climb higher to get around obstructions. It appeared that they had a destination in mind for we kept moving in a westerly direction.

We saw a lot of mule deer and it took a while for me to make them understand that I didn't care to shoot any more deer. We also scattered some javelin and saw a porcupine in a tree. By late afternoon we came to a deep box canyon - the haunt of el gato. Marcella drug the deer carcass up toward the end of the canyon and left it. Juan and I took a break and dismounted and smoked while we waited for Marcella. He rejoined us and we mounted and climbed out of the canyon and went to a small park like setting on the side of a nearby mountain. There was a spring in the park which provided adequate water for us and the horses and enough dried grass for a short stay.

We dismounted and started setting up camp for the night, following the routine of the previous night - me gathering wood, Marcella taking care of the horses, and Juan preparing to be chef. Not surprising, the menu was the same as the night before - except better. I had noticed Juan stopping several times during the day and gather plants and leaves and place them in his saddle bags. He removed them and when he packed the meat in mud he placed the herbs inside the meat along with the salt and pepper. Almost forgot, he cooked some of the back strap too. To this day I have no idea what the plant or herb was but I can testify that it gave the meat a wonderful flavor.

Before we ate, Juan was apparently scolding Marcella (in Spanish). Juan had found a bag of grain for the horses *as* he unpacked and knew that Marcella had not fed the horses the night before. So, before Marcella was allowed to eat supper he had to go feed the horses. It had already gotten dark and we had no lights but that was no problem. Both of them could move around in the dark like cats.

When Marcello returned, we all loaded our plates with meat, beans, and tortillas and sat around the camp fire and ate. Whatever the wild plant or herb was that Juan had used to flavor the meat sure gave it a wonderful taste. Of course, the fact that we skipped lunch may have also had something to do with it. We were famished.

CHAPTER 5

EL GATO

While we were eating we heard the guttural growl of a big cat in the distance. Juan and Marcella began talking in Spanish and I think they concluded that the cat had found the bait. As we were drinking coffee after eating, the coyotes began their evening concert. Words can't describe the feelings of being in such a wild and isolated place and so close to nature.

Before we turned in, the wind kicked up and the temperature started dropping - a few flakes of snow began to fall. We added a couple of large logs to the fire and crawled into our blankets - it was going to be a cold night.

I slept fast this night and woke before either of them. I slipped on my boots and jacket and built up the fire before I walked off a few yards from camp to bleed my lizard. I rummaged around and found the coffee and coffee pot, got water from the spring and had coffee brewing when Juan and Marcello got up. Juan started fixing breakfast and Marcello checked on the horses. The snow had been light, about an inch had accumulated on the ground.

The breakfast menu had changed slightly. This morning we had oats, broiled beef, and tortillas. It was good and very filling. I guessed that we would skip lunch again and we did - every day actually. After breakfast we broke camp and packed up the gear. I began to wonder why Marcello had not caught and saddled the horses. Juan tried to explain something to me but I could not understand. Then Marcello tried but no entiendo. Oh well, back to the drawing board. Marcello got a stick and began drawing pictures in the dirt and the light bulb finally flashed in my head - we were going to go check the cat bait and we would walk.

I got my Winchester and a handful of cartridge Marcello got the .22, and we started walking with Marcello in the lead. The ground wasn't completely covered with snow, there were places where the wind had cleared it and other places had small drifts. When we got near the rim of the box canyon where we had left the bait, Marcello stopped and examined the ground. Juan and I joined him and he pointed to a patch of snow. There was a huge cat track and my blood pressure started to rise.

We moved cautiously toward the edge of the rim. The last few yards we crawled and the last few feet we slithered. Even before we were able to peep over the rim we heard noises down below in the canyon; it sounded like something gnawing on bones. We carefully looked over the rim and saw the largest mountain lion in North America gorging himself on the venison we had provided. I eased the Winchester into position for a shot, cocked the hammer, drew a bead on his head, and squeezed the trigger. I heard the bullet "whack" and the big cat dropped like he had been pole axed. "Bueno" said Juan and Marcello grinned and shook my hand.

I looked back down at the cat and caught a glimpse of a coyote. The sound of the shot had frightened the coyotes but apparently they couldn't determine e source or direction of the shot. I shucked out the spent shell and jacked a live round into my rifle and took aim at a coyote - Marcello was taking aim with the .22. I fired first and my coyote dropped; an instant later the .22 cracked and another coyote bit the dust. The canyon came alive with escaping coyotes running in every direction. Marcello and I emptied our rifles before they all escaped. We killed eight coyotes - each. We reloaded and started to work our way down into the canyon. The crevice we chose to go down presented a tight squeeze but in those days I was much thinner and finally made it.

Up close, the mountain lion was much larger than he had appeared from our view on the rim. He was about eight feet long from nose to tip of tail and weighed about 300 pounds. He was an old tom and very battle scarred, particularly wounds on his head. He was missing two toes on his right front paw and three of his teeth were broken. I guessed the old boy had lived a rough life. Despite his scarred condition we decided to skin him and save his hide so we got out our knives and went to work, when we had him skinned we cut off the coyote tails and saved the skinned tails (for proof to collect the ranchers bounty). When we finished we headed back to our camp site.

When we returned to camp Juan and I rubbed salt into the pelt while Marcello rounded up the horses. When he returned with them they were very skittish and nervous; they could smell that old cat. I finished with the hide and Juan helped Marcello saddle and pack our now wild horses. It took all three of us to get the pack (which contained the hide) loaded on to the pack horse.

CHAPTER 6

SURROUNDED BY JAVELINA

It was mid morning before we were in the saddle and moving west again. The mountains were getting taller and the going was getting tougher. I really had no desire to shoot anything else - unless we stumbled upon a bear or something . We had stopped for a smoke break around noon and I suggested we stop early this day if we found a suitable camp site. Juan took the lead and around mid afternoon we came upon a wide valley and you could see the sun reflecting off what appeared to be water. We rode directly to it and it turned out to be a small manmade lake . A small stream flowed through the valley and someone had constructed a dam of rocks and dirt and formed the small lake. The lake contained maybe 4 or 5 acres. Some wild ducks flew from it as we rode up.

We dismounted, tied the horses, and walked around looking for a good camp site and exploring in general. There were a lot of tracks at water's edge - deer, cat, coyote, quail, and something that resembled a deer track only narrower. I pointed at the unfamiliar track and asked "Que esta? (What in heck is that?) and Juan said “Javelina". We found a nice flat grassy spot near the lake and started setting up camp. I gathered rocks and built a fireplace and started gathering wood for the fire. While I was gathering wood I thought I smelled smoke. But when I drug the wood into camp there was no fire?

Strange.... And Juan and Marcello seemed nervous..........Why? What in the heck is going on? (Later proved to be smoke from the stove at the Lonesome Pine Ranch).

I decided to look around so I got out my Winchester and conveyed to them that I was going hunting and would return before dark. Marcello got the .22 rifle and followed me and Juan stayed in came Marcello had not gone far from camp when we heard strange noises ahead. We froze in our tracks and listened and watched. Marcello whispered "Javelina...mirar" and pointed. Finally I saw the small black pigs coming toward us; they were in heavy brush. Out of the corner of my eye I glimpsed Marcello taking aim and with the crack of his shot the Javelina scattered in every direction. One of them was squealing and many others were popping their teeth. Although we were in no danger it was still sort of sporty when one of those little critters literally ran between your legs - gnashing his teeth as he passed. I spotted the one that was squealing; it was the one that Marcello had hit with the .22 rifle and it was far from dead so I drew a bead on it and finished it off. Marcella plunged into the brush and drug the pig out into a clearing and proceeded to field dress it. When he finished he tied the feet together and cut a small tree limb and trimmed it for a toting pole. He slid the pole between the legs and motioned for me to take hold and we toted the pig back to camp - obviously for food. When we got to camp and Juan saw the pig he said "Muy Bueno" (very good) and proceeded to skin the pig with Marcello helping some and supervising a lot.

When they finished they joined me around the camp fire and we drank coffee and smoked and conversed by sign language and picture drawing. We decided to spend a leisurely day in camp, have a pig feast tonight, and head back toward El Trebol in the morning and do some serious deer hunting closer to headquarters.

By late morning I was getting bored and decided I didn't want to spend the day in camp. I borrowed the .22 from Marcello and thought I would wander around for a couple of hours and see if I could shoot a couple of quail for tomorrow's breakfast. I walked around the lake until I came to the creek that fed it and followed the creek at a leisurely pace. Before I realized what was happening I was in the middle of another herd of Javelinas. They discovered me and acted like the previous bunch - running in every direction and popping their teeth. Another thrill but I had no desire to shoot one of them so I just stood still until they finally cleared out. Most of them ran down the creek in the direction I was heading so I made a big circle out into the pasture and away from where I thought they might be. As I moseyed across the big pasture a large coyote jumped up and went streaking toward the creek - I snapped a shot off and knocked him down. As I walked toward him a covey of quail exploded from under my feet and scared the beans out of me. I stopped and smoked a cigarette and got myself composed again. While I was smoking I saw that the coyote was trying to get up. After he fell a couple of times he started dragging himself toward the creek I took aim at his head and finished him off and decided to get serious about the quail.

Before I finished smoking I heard the quail start talking to one another and knew they would be regrouping into a covey in a few minutes. I eased over toward where they were and found a hiding place in some young mesquites and waited for them to show. It didn't take long. A quail darted from one clump of grass to another. I eased the safety off and got ready to shoot. He moved enough so I could see him and "Bang", one down and five to go. I didn't move from my concealed position and within 30 minutes had picked off five more birds. I decided that was plenty for our breakfast so I headed back to camp, after collecting the coyote tail.

When I got close to camp I could hear Juan and Marcello talking and laughing. I eased on closer and saw the reason for the merriment Marcello was tipping a bottle of an amber liquid - then he passed the bottle to Juan. They were standing under a large pine tree and on impulse I drew a bead on a pine cone and fired. The pine cone exploded and pieces of it fell on them. They jumped, pulled their revolvers, and were looking in every direction to try to locate whoever had fired. I stepped out into the open and waved and Juan waved back. I walked into camp and Juan handed the bottle to me. I took a sip of it and it set me on fire.

That was the rawest, meanest, tequila I had ever tasted. I have no idea where it came from; I had not seen it in our pack. Maybe Marcello had it stashed in his saddle bag. I gave the quail to Juan and said "breakfast" and he replied "desaundo".

Juan borrowed the .22 from me and took a shot at a pine cone high in the tree - and missed. Marcello laughed and they started talking rapidly in Spanish; it was obvious that an argument was developing. They marched off about 50 feet from the pine tree and Juan pulled his revolver and shot at a pine cone and hit it. Then Marcello took a shot at one with his revolver and missed. More conversation and Juan waved for me to join them. It appeared that Juan wanted to have a marksmanship contest He handed me his revolver and I cocked it and shot at a pine cone; didn't hit it solidly but at least nicked it. I handed the revolver back to Juan who took a snap shot at the same pine cone I had nicked but missed it. Marcello shot at it again and hit it. Juan handed me the revolver again and pointed to another pine cone which I shot at and missed. Then Marcello snapped off a quick shot at it and missed. I shot again and hit it solidly. I handed the revolver back to Juan and while he was reloading I went and got the .22 and a box of bullets. If we were going to do much shooting I knew the .45 shells were expensive and in short supply. I suggested they put their six shooters back in their holsters and we could all shoot the rifle. They agreed. I got a piece of paper from my possessions and drew a bulls eye target on it and attached it to a tree about 100 yards away. I counted out 5 bullets for each and handed the rifle to Juan. He loaded the rifle and started to take a rest on a small tree as he aimed at the target. I stopped him and made them understand we would all shoot from a standing position - no rests. Juan took his five shots and we walked to the target to examine it; he had two hits - a 9 ring and a 7 ring, I marked the holes with my ball point and we walked back to the firing line and Juan handed the rifle to Marcello who loaded and prepared to fire. Marcello fired his five rounds very rapidly. We went back to the target to examine it and he had three hits -all 5's I marked them and we marched back to the firing line. I took the rifle and loaded it and slowly fired my five rounds - taking careful aim and gently squeezing off each round. We went to the target for the third time and it was obvious who had won this contest. I had hit the target five times with 2 in the bulls eye and the other 3 in the 9 ring. Had we been able to converse I would have told them they had been beaten by the rifle shooting champion of the Commonwealth of Kentucky – circa 1949. But they beat me with the pistols.

CHAPTER 7

IT LOOKED LIKE

PANCHO VILLA HIMSELF

Darkness was slipping up on us so we built up the fire and Juan rigged some forked sticks and a spit to cook the pig over the fire after we had a good bed of hot coals. He fixed a pot of fresh coffee and we sipped coffee and smoked while the meat cooked. The meat cooking smelled good and our mouths were beginning to water. Juan turned the spit and said “Muy Bueno peeg" and I replied "Si. By now I was considering myself sort of fluent in Spanish. Juan put on some beans to warm and laid some tortillas on a stone to warm also. He grinned and asked "Tengo hombre; and I immediately responded "Si". (see how my Spanish is improving).

As usual it was dark by the time we sat down to eat supper. We got our tin plates and cups and Juan took his hunting knife and sliced off big chunks of pig and loaded our plates with pig, beans, and tortillas. Marcello poured a generous portion of the fiery picante on each plate and a big shot of tequila in each cup of coffee. Bon appetite.

We were on about our third mouthful when a very large man rode right up to the fire on his horse. He had a curled down handlebar mustache and a stubble of beard. He was wearing a large sombrero and it was cocked back on his head - as if he owned the place. But by far the most impressive thing about him was the bandoleer of bullets that hung from his shoulder and across his chest and the pair of pearl handled six guns strapped to his waist. He looked like Pancho Villa himself to me - very impressive. He said something in Spanish and Juan and Marcello started talking at once; both were obviously scared. The stranger held up his hand to silence them and Juan looked at me with pleading eyes and tried to explain the problem by sign language. As usual, I was slow in catching on but finally figured it out and went to my pack and found the note Jose had given me *as* we left the ranch. I came back to the camp fire and could see the relief in Juan's eyes when I gave him the note. He stepped around the fire and handed the note to the stranger.

The stranger swung off his horse and walked up to the fire so he could read the note. He started to smile as he was reading and I knew everything was fine. He stuck the note in his pocket, reared back and looked me over, gave a big smile and said "Mucho Gusto Senior Guillermo" he next gave me a big bear hug and looked over my shoulder at Juan and said "Mi compadre". Then he told all of us "Welcome to the Lonesome Pine - mi casa es su casa," I am Wuences Lau. Next I extended my hand for a handshake and his grip was like a vise -- I squeezed with all my strength and he grinned and said "Bueno". (I too have a powerful grip). He was a very powerful man and I was sure proud to be his friend. I could understand why Juan and Marcello had been nervous; this was one hombre you wouldn't want as an enemy. Wuences Lau went around the fire and shook hands with Juan and Marcello and they started a conversation in Spanish. I picked up a word now and then and sort of pieced what they were talking about - mostly me and Jose.

Juan and Marcello explained that we were on a hunting trip and that Don Jose had instructed them to lead me into the mountains and try to kill the big cat that had been killing some of his calves. He knew the hunt would put us on Wuences Lau's ranch - thus the note.

My interpretation was supported by them showing him the deer rack and the cat hide., and my Winchester. Wuences Lau apparently asked them about all the shooting that afternoon for Marcello retrieved the target from the tree and showed him where each of us had hit. Wuences Lau leaned back again and once more looked me over and said "Senorita Carolina has married a real hombre - bueno".

Juan got a plate and cup for Wuences Lau and generously loaded them with food and coffee - Marcello added a stiff shot of tequila to the coffee and picante to the beans and pig. We sat around the fire and finished eating; then smoked and drank coffee. Wuences Lau had borrowed a cigarette from me and really bragged on it; so I went to my pack and found the extra carton I had brought and gave it to him. He was very pleased and invited all of us to breakfast at his casa and we accepted his invitation.

We put a couple of logs on the fire and settled down for a couple of hours of smoking, drinking, and conversation. Of course I had to get a stick and draw pictures and use sign language. Never the less, I really enjoyed the fellowship. I really regretted my ignorance of the Spanish language. I'm sure that Wuences Lau could have told many interesting stories of his life in the wild Sierra Madres. It would have made a terrific book. His Lonesome Pine ranch was one of the largest cattle ranches in the State of Chihuahua and he had built it all by himself. Although he had a very rough exterior, I suspect he had a heart of gold. He invited us to spend the night at his ranch. We thanked him but told him we were really enjoying the great outdoors.

It must have been past midnight when he finally got up, said goodnight "Buena noches" and rode off We pulled our bed rolls up closer to the fire, added a couple of logs to it, and turned in for the night. It had gotten very cold.

As day broke we got up and broke camp, Marcello took care of the horses and Juan and I packed. We swung into the saddles and Juan led off in an easterly direction. A short distance from our campsite we struck a dirt road and followed it. In about twenty minutes the Lonesome Pine ranch house and headquarters came into view. The house was an imposing two story structure built of adobe and logs, sitting on the side of a mountain with a panoramic view of a large valley which was full of Herford cattle.

We smelled bacon frying, coffee brewing, and heard hound dogs barking before we reached the house. We rode into the yard, dismounted, tied our horses and climbed the steps to the porch. Wuences Lau met us at the door and invited us inside. When he introduced us I got another bear hug from him and a hug and kiss from his wife. A radio was blaring Mariachi music so loud you couldn't talk. Wuences Lau bellowed something and the Chinese cook scurried from the kitchen and turned the volume down. I looked around the house; it was very imposing. The furniture was massive - Mexican colonial style. There were many pictures, some hanging on the walls and some framed and sifting on chests, etc. Senora Lau showed me a picture of Don Jose's family, including my wife who was about 12 at the time the picture was made, and another picture of my wife riding a horse when she was about 16. She explained that my wife was an excellent rider - as good as any man. (That was good to know, in case we ever owned horses and a ranch of our own - which we finally did late in life).

They escorted us to the dining room and we were seated. Soon the cook arrived with a huge platter of fried bacon and chorizo. He went back to the kitchen and returned with a platter of fried eggs and another of flour tortillas. There was a bowl of picante sauce on the table, not nearly as hot *as the sauce* I had become accustomed to - but good. Also, there was a jar of wild mountain honey on the table. It was excellent. This was truly another memorable meal.

After we finished the meal we sat and drank coffee and smoked and visited. We were getting ready to leave when Senora Lau said something and left the room. She returned in a couple of minutes with a camera and had us pose for several pictures. She had Juan take a picture of me with her and Wuences Lau - I thought the title to this photo will be "the new gringo addition to the family". But I didn't mind, it was a fine family to join.

CHAPTER 8

INDIAN VILLAGE

I didn't think we ever going to "escape" the Lonesome Pine ranch house. Every time we got up to leave something was said and they got into another long winded conversation. Obviously not many visitors made it to this remote ranch and they were starved for conversation. (again, I regretted I couldn't speak their language - we would have spent the day). When we finally made it outside to our horses, a large gathering of the ranch workers had gathered to look us over. We swung into the saddle and had started across the yard when Senora Lau yelled from the porch and came running toward me. She came right up to my horse and handed me a flour sack which was fully packed. I thanked her and nudged the mare with a spur and we loped off amidst shouts of last minute conversation. We stayed on the dirt road for about ten miles and finally turned off into another big valley and headed toward the sun (east). There was a stream in the valley and we stopped for water and a smoke break. My wrist ached from holding the heavy sack and I opened it to check the contents. As I suspected, it contained food - a slab of bacon, eggs wrapped in paper and packed inside a jar, a jar of mountain honey, a jar of cooked stew and a jar of picante, plus a sack full of cookies (bescotches) and a small sack of pinion nuts. We ate a few cookies and I repacked everything in the saddle bags.

We remounted and continued through the valley and when it began to narrow we climbed up the east side of it and went through a gap and dropped down on a large flat plateau on the other side. We had ridden perhaps five miles across the plateau when I saw a huge rock (large as a four story building) jutting up high above ground level. Juan saw me looking at it and said "ciudad los indios". That sounded very interesting so I turned the mare and rode toward the big rock and they followed. When we got to the rock we dismounted and tied the horses and started to walk around the base of the rock Juan stopped and picked up something and handed it to me and I said "arrowhead". He responded: Parta da fletcha." We continued walking around the rock and I watched the ground and found a couple more perfectly shaped flint arrowheads. We came to an overhang and there was the remains of a very ancient camp fire and lying helter skelter around were hollowed rocks apparently made from lava and sausage shaped flint rocks (metates). These rocks were used to grind corn. I am a rock hound by birth I suppose and this place was heavenly. I continued to explore all around this massive rock but could not find any way to climb up on it. There is no telling what lay hidden in the ledges high above our heads. In my ground level exploring I found several more arrowheads and a tomahawk head. I loaded all of my rocks in the saddle bags of the horses. Juan and Marcello did not seem too pleased that I was carting off so many artifacts from their ancestors, the ancient ones. (I have always wanted to return to this ancient Indian Village but I'm sure I could not locate it any more - Jose, Juan, & Marcello have long since passed on from this earth and my memory is not what it once was). Anyway, the El Trebol has been sold.

By now it was mid afternoon and I could tell that they wanted to get moving. The artifacts did not interest them. I reluctantly climbed aboard "El Cabayo" and followed them. Just before dark we came upon a fence and crossed it, we were back on El Trebol. We swung to the left and rode to a windmill with a tank and stopped there to make camp for the night. There wasn't any wood in the vicinity so we tied the pack horse to the windmill and rode off in different directions to gather firewood. I found a dead mesquite tree and tied a rope to it and drug it back to camp. In a few minutes they rode in, each dragging a dead mesquite. Juan and I unpacked and Marcello took care of the horses.

I built the fire and Juan cooked the quail I had shot the day before which were supposed to be for breakfast. He also heated the jar of stew that el Senora Lau had given us and some tortillas; and of course made the usual pot of coffee. I noted the absence of beans (which I had grown quite fond of).

While Juan was cooking I decided to take a sponge bath and at least change underwear - I was getting sort of rank. I dug around in my pack and found a small bar of motel soap and some clean socks that I would use for a wash cloth and clean underwear and headed for the tank. It was very cold but we had been outside for so long that I was acclimated to the cold and took my bath and changed underwear just like at home. I almost decided to shave - almost. When I got back to the campfire they made some comment about how nice I smelled and started laughing. I think they said something about the girls at the bordello - who knows?

We got our plates and cups, filled them with food, and sat around the campfire to eat. The stew was exceptionally good - especially the onions, potatoes, and carrots. There had not been many vegetables in our diet as of late. The moon was full that night and the coyotes really had a concert - they were everywhere. After we rolled up in our bedrolls they continued to serenade us as we drifted off to dreamland. I lay there thinking about the pioneers who settled the west; this trip had given me a much better understanding of how their lives must have been. I had a much greater appreciation for our forefathers now.

CHAPTER 9

MAS VENADO

We were wakened the next morning by the cattle which had come to the tank to drink. We rolled out of our bedrolls and got the fire going and the coffee brewing. Juan surprised us for breakfast; we had juevos rancheros (he put the eggs to good use). We had our usual limited conversation but I picked up enough to know they were planning on arriving back at ranch headquarters tomorrow afternoon. I told them I would like to shoot a few deer to take back to the ranch for food. They nodded agreement. I asked how many we could pack ? Juan thought "cinco" but Marcello thought "seis". I agreed with Marcello - three on the pack horse and one on each riding horse.

Juan suggested that if we stayed at this water some deer would show up soon to drink - Marcello agreed. I got my Winchester and walked to the windmill and climbed up about ten feet from ground level so I had a commanding view of the countryside. Sure enough, as I scanned the surrounding pasture I counted eight deer who were grazing and working toward the water tank. There was one good 8 point buck, a spike, and 6 does in my tally. I decided to take the spike and one doe. I waited patiently for them to get closer. They were very skittish - probably smelled our camp fire and/or saw Juan and Marcello who were busy breaking camp.

In a few minutes the spike had moved within 125 yards of the tank and one of the doe's was no more than 50 yards out. I drew a bead on the spike and squeezed the trigger and he dropped. The doe froze but bounded away when I jacked another shell in the chamber. I drew a bead on the back of her head and on the next jump I pulled the trigger and she also fell. I signaled to the cowboys that I had killed 2 deer so they started toward the windmill. I climbed down and met them and led them to the deer. We pulled both of them close to the tank and cleaned them. Then we cleaned up and had a smoke before loading them on to the horses and moving out.

Marcello took the lead and was going north but I was reasonably sure that headquarters was east so I pointed east and asked "Casa?". Juan said "Si" then pointed north and said "Mas Venados". I nodded and we rode in silence for about two hours across generally open pasture with an occasional clump of mesquites. The gramma grass was brown but appeared to be in good shape. The cattle we saw were in good shape. We crossed several cattle trails which led to the windmills and tanks. We probably saw a thousand head of cattle - but no deer. Matter of fact, the only wild game we saw was a few coveys of quail. I was beginning to question their judgment in coming to this part of the ranch to hunt. But my doubts were not well founded for the terrain began to change. We came to an area that contained low hills, valleys and arroyos, thick brush and lots of mesquite trees. Instead of windmills there were several stock tanks that had been built by damming ditches. When we stopped at a tank I saw many deer tracks at water's edge. Yep, Mas Venados for certain. We rode through a few areas which I would describe as deer parks and deer were bounding away from us in every direction.

We finally rode up to a tank that contained about an acre of water and Juan said "camp" (he was beginning to pick up a few words of English). We unpacked the gear and set up camp. While we were doing this Marcella tugged at my sleeve and whispered "Venado" and pointed to a 6 point buck that was standing about a hundred yards away - watching us. I eased over and slid my Winchester out of the scabbared, quietly cocked the hammer and took rest on a mesquite tree and squeezed off a shot. He dropped and didn't move. I had aimed at his head. I looked at Marcello and pointed to a spot on my forehead (right between my eyes) to indicate where I thought he was hit Marcello looked as if he doubted so we walked to the deer and he grasped an antler and lifted the head to examine it. Sure enough, the bullet had hit right between the eyes. Marcello ginned and started to field dress the deer. We carried him back to camp and hung him in a mesquite tree. The temperature had climbed considerably so we propped the cavity open with a stick so he would chill out.

I decided to take two more deer and then we could head for the house. I figured we were about a day's ride from headquarters - maybe less. The deer were so plentiful that I knew that I could lay around camp all day and easily pick off a couple more deer. But that didn't sound like much fun so I decided to take the rifle and hunt on foot and do some exploring at the same time. I picked up my rifle and stuffed a hand full of shells in my pocket and told them I would be back in the afternoon and Juan tried to tell me something about "piscados" which I could not understand. After a drawing session on our knees in the dirt I figured it out. The tank we were camping by contained fish and they would catch some fish while I hunted. I remembered that I had a couple of rigged fishing lines packed in my "survival gear" so I dug them out and gave them to Juan before I left.

I hardly got out of camp before a couple of deer jumped up and bounded away - both were does. I didn't shoot. I had decided that the only thing I would shoot at on this sashay would be a trophy buck I would wait till I got back to camp and do any meat hunting close to camp. It was a glorious afternoon and I was enjoying the country and my "exploring" more than doing any serious hunting. I thought, not many humans have made tracks where I am traveling - not ever. I kept watching the ground, looking for arrowheads, etc. I found a couple.

I had crossed four or five arroyos and came to a wide and deep canyon. As I worked my way down into the canyon I heard a crashing in the brush below me. I stopped to try to see what had made the noise and whatever it was also stopped - it was quiet. I found a large rock and threw it in the direction of the noise and a crashing through the brush followed. I finally got a look *at* him - a huge mule deer! I decided to try to take him so I worked my way into a position that had a clear view of the floor of the canyon. I found some more rocks and kept chunking at him until I drove him out into the open on the canyon floor; then I shot at him..once, twice, three times. I thought I had hit him at least once, maybe more, but he kept running down the canyon. I remembered the lesson Marcello had taught me so I lit a cigarette and prepared to wait a while before tracking him.

After about fifteen minutes, I dropped on down into the canyon and searched the area and soon found blood that contained air bubbles. Hit in the lungs I thought as I tracked him down the canyon. I hadn't gone too far when I heard noise ahead and caught a glimpse of him. He was trying to get up so I snapped off a quick shot and heard the bullet whack so I didn't think he was going anywhere. I walked on down to him and he was real dead.

When I got up close to the deer he looked big as a horse. I lifted his head and examined his rack --sixteen points (both sides). Then reality set in - I felt like the dog that chased cars and finally caught one - what do I do now coach? I was about an hour from camp in very rugged terrain and this big deer was much too heavy for me to handle, regardless of the terrain. I did the best I could to field dress him and using a short piece of rope I carried I got his head and four quarters off the ground and tied to a tree limb. I also propped his cavity open with a stick so he could chill out It was cold enough there was no danger of the meat spoiling. I had no choice but to return to camp for help.

Before I headed for camp I climbed the tree I hung the deer in and tied my handkerchief as high in the tree as I could safely reach. Then I had a cigarette and thought things out before proceeding. First, I didn't want to get lost and second I wanted to be able to return to this spot and retrieve the deer. There really weren't any prominate landmarks to use so I decided to use my built in compass/computer: (I had recently finished navigation training in the Air Force). I figured I was now east/southeast from camp. The canyon that I was in was much larger than any canyons I had crossed when I left camp and it ran almost north/south. I headed south down toward the mouth of the canyon and at the first opportunity I turned out of the canyon and headed west. Out ahead of me was a small hill which I climbed and rested when I reached the top - facing west. I thought I could detect a plume of smoke on the horizon and I gazed intently at it. Yes, I finally convinced myself- that is smoke and I was sure it came from the campfire. I headed toward the smoke and in about an hour I made it into our camp. Camp was deserted but a pot of coffee sat near the fire so I put it on the coals and warmed it up and had myself a cup of it. While I was sipping coffee I heard Juan yell. I jumped up and headed in the direction of his shout.

I was following the water's edge and as I rounded a bend there was Juan and Marcello; Juan was holding a catfish and Marcello was examining it. I walked up to them and said "Bueno Piscado" and they smiled and Marcello went to the lake and returned with a stringer containing six more catfish - all about a pound each. Juan strung his latest catch and as he did so I explained to them that I had shot a large deer and needed help in getting him back to camp.

It was getting late in the afternoon so we decided that Marcello would get the horses and help me find my deer and bring him to camp and that Juan would stay in camp and fix a catfish dinner. Bueno! Marcello and I mounted up and I led off toward the canyon. We found the canyon and I led us straight to the tree with the deer hanging in it (plus my handkerchief which Marcello saw and thought it was a neat idea). I was right proud of my navigation. We dismounted and loaded the deer onto the pack horse. Marcello said he was "Muy Grande" and I agreed. We headed back to camp.

We could smell fish cooking before camp came into view. It made my

mouth water- that fish was going to taste good after the steady red meat diet. We rode in to camp, unloaded the big deer and strung him up in a tree, and unsaddled the horses and hobbled them. Juan motioned that supper was ready so Marcello & I went to the lake and cleaned up before gabbing our plates for the fish fry. By the time we loaded our plates, Juan was already eating. Soon, what appeared at first as a surplus of fish, turned out to be
insufficient. The fish was gone and Marcello was complaining there was not enough and blaming Juan for throwing a couple of smaller fish they had caught back into the lake.

We cleaned the plates and had a final cup of coffee and a smoke and I told them I was going to sleep. I had done a lot of walking that day and was tired - the old bedroll felt real good. I could hear them talking quietly as I drifted off to sleep.

I awoke late the next morning; the sun was already peeping over the horizon. Juan and Marcello were drinking coffee by the fire; they had already finished breakfast. I crawled out of the sack, got dressed and joined them. They had decided to let me catch up on my sleep the last night in camp. Juan started making preparations to fix my breakfast but I stopped him. I went to the pack and got a piece of jerky and a handful of bescoches (cookies). That would be my breakfast.

While I was chewing the jerky I looked toward the tank and saw two does walking down the hill toward the water. I signaled for Juan to hand me my rifle and he did. I drew a bead on the largest doe and fired - she dropped. I decided not to shoot at the other doe - the hunt was over so I just watched as she bounded up the hill.

I finished breakfast and went to the doe and field dressed her while Juan & Marcello broke camp and packed up. The doe was small so I lifted her onto my shoulder and carried her back into camp. Marcello tied her on the pack horse, behind the large mule deer, and we climbed into the saddles and headed for ranch headquarters. We rode steadily all morning and entered the gate at the ranch compound around 2 p.m. Everyone came out to examine our trophies and both Juan and Marcello started telling them all about our great hunt I slipped away and took a warm bath, shaved, and put on clean clothes and felt like a new man. You really don't appreciate some of the simple things - until you do without them for a few days.

Don Jose came in and asked me how I enjoyed the hunt and I said "Muy Bueno". He smiled at my new found Spanish. I said, "Jose, I don't want to pry but out of curiosity, how large is El Trebol and Lonesome Pine and how many cattle are on each?" He thought for a second before answering and said "The Lonesome Pine is one of the largest ranches in Mexico - it contains about 400 sections (1 section is 640 acres - therefore it contained about 256,000 acres) and probably had 12,000 to

15,000 head of cattle on it. Then I asked again "El Trebol?" He said "By comparison , El Trebol is small; about half the size of Lonesome Pine. That explained why we could hunt for a week on horseback and never get off "family" land.

That night another big fire was built outside and we had another fiesta I wasn't hungry for meat so I ate a few chicken and cheese Enchilada's and washed them down with dos exes cervesa. Juan made a little speech to the group and told them what a great hunter I was and what a good time we had on our hunt. The band and singers sung some Christmas carols that were beautiful. When the music stopped I was expected to make a speech to the gathering so I climbed upon the "stage" with the band and made this short speech:

Senores, senores, Mi compadres:

Jose translated to Spanish for me.

Thank you for the most wonderful week of my life. I shall always cherish the memory of this week. I capped the ceremony by giving my guns, knife, and ammo, to Juan and Marcello and my camera and film to Juan's wife. (With this gesture I moved from great hunter to super hero status).

Don Jose and I excused ourselves early and slipped to his quarters and went to bed. We planned to leave early the next day.

CHAPTER 10

THE FINAL CHAPTER - THE TRIP HOME

We arose early the next morning, got dressed, and ate a ranch breakfast which Juan's wife prepared for us. Then we started getting ready to leave. The packing and preparations were not nearly as elaborate as on the trip down. Since I had given my guns to the cowboys there was no reason to hide anything on the trip back.

Don Jose was taking a side of beef back and I was taking two sets of deer antlers and some arrowheads and artifacts. We just threw everything in a tarp, rolled it up and threw it in the bed of the pickup. We still had two cases of peaches and a carton of cigarettes for barter, if necessary, on the return trip.

The weather remained crisp and cold and it had not rained so we didn't anticipate any problems on the dirt road. We filled the truck and the extra tanks with gasoline, said our goodbyes, crawled in the pickup and headed northward. Jose and I were talking and having so much fun that we were driving into La Mula before I realized it. We had been traveling over three hours.

We stopped at the same store in La Mula Jose said they had excellent wild honey so we went inside and bought a couple of jars of it. I also bought a bottle of vanilla which smelled fabulous, a loaf of pan, and a huge chunk of cheese. We were ready to leave and Jose found a couple of cold colas somewhere in the store plus a large sack of raw peanuts. Listo! Time to go. When we stepped outside we were in for a big surprise!!!! The truck was surrounded by a Mariachi band - musical instruments, sombreros and all.

The band leader approached Jose and asked if he would transport them to Ojinaga - he offered to pay 100 pesos for the trip. He explained they had played for a wedding and fiesta in La Mula the night before and the autobus which had brought them down was broken down and they did not know when it would be fixed. All he knew was that it was two day till Christmas and they were stranded.

Jose listened to everything the band leader said and when he finished Jose said “No, I will not take you and your band to Ojinaga for 100 pesos, or 20 pesos either. All their faces dropped, they were a sad looking lot. Then Jose spoke again" I'll make you a proposition - I'll agree to take you if you promise to play JESUS IN CHIAHUA all the way there and further agree to put on a full hour concert of Christmas music for the poor people and free of charge when we arrive "A cheer went up along with a resounding "Si,Si".

Jose said "load" and the musicians started to climb aboard most of their instruments were hanging over the side. Jose started the truck and we moved off slowly but had not gone three blocks when he stopped.

He told them if they did not play as agreed they must get off and walk. There was a mad scramble for instruments and soon the sweet strains of JESUS IN CHIHUA were floating from the bed of Jose's pickup truck. Except for a brief rest stop we traveled steadily down the dusty dirt road. When we reached the check point we were greeted by all the soldiers who had heard us coming. They were dancing in the road and singing and cheering. One of the soldiers walked up to the truck and inquired if we had any contraband and Jose said "Si". The soldier got excited and asked "what is it?" and Jose replied "the band". Everyone got a big laugh out of this, including the soldier. Jose asked "Where is El Jefe?" but before anyone could answer El Jefe yelled as he rounded the corner of the adobe building. Jose and I got out and met him *as* he approached the truck. He embraced Jose first then gave me another bear hug. They talked for a minute and Jose got a case of peaches from the truck. El Jefe said that was not necessary- the music *was* enough. Jose instructed me to bring the side of beef so we look beef and peaches into the building and left them. Jose announced "four more songs and we must leave- what are your requests". The band leader selected four of the requests and they started playing them. When they got to the fourth song you would never guess what it was (clue - it was the most requested song) Jose started the truck and we pulled away slowly as the band played its most robust version of JESUS IN.

We continued down the dusty, bumpy road. I made us some cheese sandwiches which we ate and washed down with water from Jose's extra large canteen that stayed in the truck at all times. We made one more rest stop and by mid afternoon were parking at the square in Ojinaga. Jose let the band members walk around, drink cokes and eat snacks for about ten minutes before the concert started (meantime he found some young boys who he gave quarters to so they could spread the word around about the free concert. By the time the music started, we had drawn a crowd. The crowd kept getting larger with each song and at the end of the hour it was a huge crowd. After the last song the band leader told the crowd that the music was compliments of Don Jose Nieto. The crowd started a chant - Viva Don Jose! Viva Don Jose! It was really something.

Jose had slipped off to a store before the band quit playing and bought a huge bag full of dulces so before we left he climbed into the bed of the truck and threw handful after handful of candy to the children in the crowd. Some came forward and he handed them all the candy they wanted. He was truly a very generous man.

We drove across the bridge and were soon parked in the driveway and entering his house. His wife embraced him and my wife embraced me and asked "How was the trip?" I said "It was one of my most memorable experiences" (and it remains so to this day - some 55 years later). The end.

ALASKAN SMORGASBOARD

(A FISHING ADVENTURE)

CHAPTER 1

PLANNING THE TRIP

Dewey Lawhon and I were partners in an accounting practice in Dallas. Both of us loved to fish and we had many good ole boy clients who also loved to fish. Late one afternoon in the winter of 1982 the intercom in my office buzzed and when I answered it Dewey said " Drop whatever you are doing and come to my office - we've got something really important to talk about". I started down the hall wondering what sort of emergency might have arisen - it was near year end and about time for "emergencies". I reached Dewey's office and stepped inside and there sat Tom Williams, a client, who was grinning like a possum in a cow carcass. With Tom's smile and Dewey's smile I relaxed immediately - I knew there was no emergency this time.

I sat down and Dewey in his slow Arkansas drawl asked" How would you like to go fishing in Alaska?" I answered, "I'd like that" and Tom grinned more and said "kinda thought you would - my son (John) is working on the Alaska pipeline and I talked to him last night and he said if I could get seven men together willing to pay around 6 or 7 thousand each, he would take care of all the details for a fishing trip to Alaska". I said "count me in". Dewey said you, me, and Tom makes three - we need to come up with four more; any ideas? I said "You know that won't be a problem- the problem will be those we don't invite who get mad". He nodded. Dewey said" Since John will be doing all the work and taking care of all the details, it is not fair for him to have to pay a full share" Tom and I agreed and added, " If you tell everyone on the front end they are paying a part of John's share of the cost, it won't be a problem."

Tom had been to Alaska to visit John in August and he showed us a bunch of photos made on the trip. The scenery was fantastic and the fish were large. We really got excited at the thought of catching those huge fish and mentioned we could close the office and leave immediately. Tom said "won't work" and went on to explain there was a very short period of time when the weather would permit open water fishing. He said that period *was* basically July and August. The exact dates of our trip would be dictated by the dates we could rent a camp, sign up guides, etc things that John would take care of. All we needed to do was line up four more fisherman and send John some money for deposits, etc. Tom and I appointed Dewey treasurer for the trip.

We tried to call John from Deweys office but were unable to reach him. Dewey was concerned. Tom said "Heck fire, its only December 16th, we got at least seven months. Dewey said, "We need to know the dates before we start calling people". Tom said, "I'll be talking to John in a week or so and I'll tell him to go ahead and book for eight and let us know the dates *as* soon as possible". Dewey asked "Won't he need money for deposits?" Tom said "Don't worry about that, he's making more money than he can spend right now, let him use some of it". Dewey said "I won't argue with you - and winked at me"

We talked fishing for an hour or so and Tom really had us excited with his tales of all the large fish he and John had caught last summer. Dewey asked, "What all do we need to take". Tom mentioned a long list of stuff but recommended we wait and let John give us a list of things to bring, he knew John would buy a lot of the stuff in Anchorage and we wouldn't have to fool with it - for example, insect repellent. He added "the only thing for sure I know you will need is a good fly rod and waders". Tom had to leave and Dewey and I sat and fished some more until he finally said " Lets walk over to Cullum & Boren (a ritzy downtown sporting goods store) and look at fly rods and stuff I said "let's go" but had already made up my mind that I would wait until John told us what to bring and then I would order mine from Cabellos - I still had the last catalog they had sent for Christmas.

When we got to the store we stopped and admired the display in the front window. It was an African scene complete with stuffed lions and all plus stuff you might need on safari. I gulped when I saw the price tag on the rifle the mannequin was holding - $4,750. No doubt this was an expensive place to shop. We went inside and were met by a distinguished looking gentleman. (I kept thinking he reminds me more of a butler than a salesman). Dewey told him we were going fishing in Alaska so he escorted us to the fishing equipment. We started looking at their fly rods first; they were all high quality split bamboo rods and priced from $200 to $1,000. Not really my idea of a fishing pole. Dewey selected one of the mid price range rods - I just looked. We next looked at the flies, spinning lures and accessories. The salesman selected a group of flies and lures which he personally recommended for fishing Alaskan waters. (I would bet my hat he had never been near Alaskan waters - matter of fact I'd also bet my other hat that he wasn't even a fisherman). Made no difference, Dewey took what he selected but didn't stop there - he selected a fishing vest, hat, waders, and jacket to add to his purchase. The salesman was getting ready to ring the sale when Dewey said "what about a fly reel and spinning rod and reel". The salesman said absolutely, we mustn't forget that" so Dewey selected those items plus lines; then he was ready to check out. The salesman rang it up and it came to a little over $1,200 and Dewey handed him a credit card.

I had selected a couple of flies called "scaup" which I remembered reading about in an Outdoor Life article on Alaska so I gave them to the salesman to ring up. They came to a whole $5.00 and I handed him an Abe Lincoln and he gave me a haughty look I was glad to get out of that store and back into the fresh air.

As we walked back to the office I commented "At this rate, this could be a very expensive trip. He said "You only live once - may as well enjoy it".

Tom called the next day and said he had talked to John - twice. He called John and told him we were coming but needed to know the exact dates. John called back later and told him we were booked for seven days of lodging and fishing commencing July 18th (a Sunday) Actually, the fishing would start on Monday the 19th and end on a Saturday the 24th. Tom also told us to get only three more fishermen for the trip. He said his cousin, Wallace Purdue, of Nashville had called and said he wanted to go and he told him he could. Dewey and I got on the phone and called a couple of clients who might want to go and the first three that we talked to "signed up". They were Eddie Pelt and Don Cutter from Duncanville and Roy Ralls from Fort Worth and each of them promised to send a $3,000 deposit immediately - which they did.

Dewey next started shopping for air transportation round trip; to

Anchorage. The best deal he came up with was a Braniff flight to Calgary coupled with a Northwest flight from Calgary to Anchorage. He booked seven reservations so all we had to do now was wait for July 16th to arrive.

In a few weeks we received a letter from John. In his letter he confirmed the lodging reservations at Lake Clark Lodge and the guide service, including float planes, with the Lake Clark Guide Service. He also confirmed our hotel reservations at the Hyatt in Anchorage for July 17th as well as the charter flight from Anchorage to Lake Clark. Everything was now cast in stone. We were excited but knew it was going to be a long wait. John's letter also included a check list of things to bring- basically the same stuff that Tom had already told us except he added flashlight, camera, and loads of film. We called the other three and set up a meeting in our office to go over plans , hand out lists, etc. Everyone showed up the following Tuesday as planned and we planned and talked and bragged. Dewey pulled out the stuff he had purchased and showed it to them and they were impressed - especially at the price tags. Roy said he wanted to go to that store after the meeting and Dewey agreed to take him. Eddie asked me if I had bought my stuff yet. I told him I planned to order it in a day or two. He said he had ordered some stuff from the Bass Pro Shop and wanted to know if that was where I planned to order from. I told him that I would order from Cabellos and explained they catered to northern fishermen. Don asked if he could borrow the catalog and I promised to mail it to him.

I sat down that night with the Cabellos catalog and ordered basically the same stuff that Dewey had bought and it cost around $300. I hasten to add, my fly rod was spun glass instead of split bamboo and my reels were Ambassadors instead of Orvis. But when it came down to the acid test - catching fish - they worked just fine.

When my order arrived, I unpacked it and laid it out for inspection. I now had a fly rod with automatic fly reel, floating and sinking fly lines, leaders, weights, large assortment of flies and small plastic boxes to store them in, fly fishing vest, spinning rod and reel, spinning lures, waders, hat with mosquito net, flashlight, and plastic tubes to carry my rods in. I was ready for whatever Alaska had to offer.

That summer I spent many hours in the back yard, practicing fly casting I had used a fly rod in my youth and caught many bream and bass on one so I was not a complete novice. As a matter of fact, by the end of summer I could drop a fly within a couple of inches of where I aimed. *I* even went bass fishing a couple of times and took only the fly rod. The bass fishermen thought I was crazy - until they watched me land a couple of fish.

I packed and repacked my stuff several limes that summer. Time seemed to drag. ..I didn't think July 16th would ever roll around. Finally, the July 4th holiday came and went and the magic day ,Friday July 16th did arrive. We were scheduled to depart Love Field at 1 pm. That morning I carefully packed for the final time and got to the airport by 11 am and I was the last of the group there. We were as excited as kids at Christmas. We had lunch at the airport and our wives left. They were tired of hearing about fishing. Next, we went to the baggage check in and got rid of our baggage and then to the gate for boarding, but no one was there. We checked the time - 12:15, a little early yet. At 12:44 a uniformed employee arrived and checked us in. Seat assignments were academic, we were the only passengers on the flight. In a couple of minutes we boarded the big jet and sat down. I sat down by Wallace and decided I would try to get to know him a little - I already knew everyone else.

In a few minutes the big bird started moving and soon was shooting down the runway. It finally broke gravity's hold on it and we were airborne - North to Alaska.

CHAPTER 2

THE TRIP UP

Since we had the plane to ourselves, we got plenty of attention. Roy bought a round of drinks, then Dewey, then Eddie, then me. With each round of drinks the fishing tales became more difficult to believe. An outsider would have thought we were all professional tournament fishermen. Before things got completely out of hand the hostess served food and insisted we eat; all of us were beginning to get just a wee bit drunk. She refused to serve any more alcohol, after she cleared the treys and before we got back on the juice the pilot came on the inner com and announced we would be landing in Calgary in fifteen minutes. We had our last smokes and fastened our seat belts. It had been a smooth flight and seemed short. I'm sure everyone thought as I; shoot fire we'll be in Alaska in a couple of hours.

However, after we deplaned we wandered all over the Calgary airport, looking for Northwest Airlines flight 636. No one could find it and the airport was nearly deserted.

Don finally found someone who told him that flight 636 had been cancelled but there would be another flight to Anchorage at 7 am. We assumed they would book us on it This turn of events put a damper on our spirits and Dewey suffered a lot of verbal abuse for the travel arrangements; although he had nothing to do with the cancelled flight. It was obvious we were in for a long night at a semi-deserted airport. We split up to see what we could scrounge up. When we regrouped we had a pot of coffee and a deck of cards - don't ask where they came from. We started playing cards and drinking coffee - there wasn't any other choice. Tom dropped out of the penny poker game soon and curled up in a lounge seat and went to sleep.

I too became bored with the game and got up and stretched and started to wander around the terminal once more. I looked *at* my watch and saw that it *was* nearly 12pm, no wonder this place was deserted. I was standing there smoking a cigarette when I saw two fairly attractive ladies come in the front door and walk across the terminal and get on an elevator. Strange. I hadn't seen the elevator before and did not realize the terminal had a second floor.

I walked across the terminal and pushed the up button on the elevator and rode up a floor and got off I heard music and talking down the hall and walked down to find its source. And there before my eyes was an Admirals Club. I had done a considerable amount of air travel in years past and had been a member of the fine American Airlines club at one time; although I had no idea as to my current status. I pulled out my wallet and sorted through credit cards, etc. and found an old rat eared Admirals Club card and marched up to the door and punched the buzzer. In moments the door opened and I was met by a lovely middle aged hostess. Behind her were dozens of people - the place was packed. I showed her my card and explained the situation. She was quite sympathetic and said "Of course we were welcome-all of us". I told her we would gladly pay. She said they would run a tab for the drinks but everything else was complimentary.

I went back downstairs to get the gang. When I walked up to the poker game Roy said "Where the heck have you been - loan me some money". I gave him a quizzical look and he explained they had gotten bored with penny poker and had raised to table stakes and that Eddie had almost cleaned everyone out and wouldn't cash a check or accept credit cards. I got the drift - everyone except Eddie was frowning. I said "I've been upstairs to a party." Dewey asked "Where?" and I said "Admirals Club". Everyone pulled out their wallets and looked - and none of them were members. Roy observed " You must have a membership-right?" Yep" says I, but I can only take one guest at a time. I told them we would cut the cards to determine the priority of visits. Eddie said "I’ve got a better idea- since I'm a big client of your firm, let me have that damn card if you want to retain my business". Dewey looked me in the eye and said "You had better do it". (I knew there would be trouble sooner or later from this bunch of high rollers). I looked at Eddie and said "Screw you" and added, "if you will cash checks for the boys you cleaned out and agree to pick up the bar tab, I'll take all of you back up there as my guests. Eddie said "OK" "But you said the rule was one guest only" "Rules can be broken if you smile just right " I said. Everyone jumped up from the card game and followed me to the elevator and we went up to the second floor. I touched the buzzer at the club and the sweet lady I had talked to opened the door and greeted us and escorted us to a table - she sat down with us and signaled a waiter who came and took our orders. Eddie let it be known that he would take care of the tab. Soon everyone was relaxed and in a party mood. A couple of the guys started flirting with our hostess but she was accustomed to such behavior and didn't seem to mind. I overheard Eddie ask "Is it true that a member is allowed only one guest?" She said "Yes, that is the rule - however I made an exception in your case because you are stranded and also because of his infectious Texas smile". I stifled a chuckle when I saw the look on Eddie's face.

We ordered sandwiches and a couple more rounds of drinks. Everyone was having a good time and Don had taken the initiative and danced with a lady at another table. In an hour Don had convinced the ladies at the other table to join us. There were four of them and they all wanted to dance. The hostess reappeared and asked "Is one of you named Dewey Lawhon?". Dewey stood up and said "Yes ma'am - but I must not have made much of an impression on you when I introduced myself a couple of hours ago". She said "I'm sorry, I meet so many strangers and have difficulty remembering names - the reason I inquired is because security called from downstairs and said there is a man down there who is desperately looking for you". We all said in unison "Tom must have woke up" and then laughed. I could just envision what it must have been like when he woke up and all of us were gone - He probably thought we had abandoned him and gone on to Alaska.

Dewey went downstairs and retrieved poor ole Tom. Tom had a couple of stiff drinks and soon forgot his scare. At 2am the hostess told us they were closing the club. We asked if there was any way we could stay until 7am? She said "Only if one of the employees is willing to stay with you". Eddie spoke up and said "There's a hundred dollar bill waiting for the volunteer". She said "Let me go check" and left. Moments later she returned with Kevin, the bartender , and said he would stay with us. We thanked her and she left and locked the front door on the way out. Kevin put on a pot of coffee and Tom took over a couch and went back to sleep. We drank coffee and talked for awhile and one by one left the group and found a chair or sprawled out on the carpet and went to sleep. Kevin woke us at

6 am and had a fresh pot of coffee made. We had our coffee, went to the washroom, and then went downstairs to board the plane. By five after seven we were back in the air and headed for Anchorage. This flight was different from our first leg - there were about twenty additional passengers aboard, mostly Orientals.

CHAPTER 3

ANCHORAGE, ALASKA

Most of our group slept as we flew across Canada - it had been a long and mostly sleepless night in Calgary. I had a window seat and was fascinated by the scenery below and couldn't sleep. Finally the plane altered its heading and was heading west and starting to descend and soon we were over water- the Gulf of Alaska. In a few minutes we landed and John was there to meet us as we got off the plane. We waited for our luggage then caught cabs to the Hilton. After we checked in and deposited our luggage in our rooms we rejoined John who loaded us into his Suburban and took us on a sightseeing tour of the city.

One thing noticeable was the tremendous number of airplanes; they were everywhere and most of them were float planes. It seemed that every puddle of water had a plane sitting in it. John explained that there were very few highways in Alaska and that the primary mode of transportation was the float plane. He said there were more planes in Alaska than cars and it certainly looked that way. John referred to the planes as Alaskan pickups. After we drove around a while we ended up in the downtown area and parked the vehicle and continued our tour on foot. We went into many shops and bought a lot of Alaskan stuff-

carvings out of whalebones, gold jewelry, Eskimo dolls, etc. Next we went to a topless bar called the Trading Post or some such name. There were several Alaskan sourdoughs in there, busily drinking and stuffing bills in the girls G strings. We had a couple of drinks and watched the activities for awhile and decided it was time for supper.

John led us up the street to a restaurant which he said was famous for its seafood- particularly Alaskan king crab. I don't remember the name of the place but I do remember the delicious meal I had there - crab over linguini covered with a perfect Alfredo sauce. Excellent!!! Tom, Wallace, and John decided to party some more but the rest of us opted for sleep, even though it was still daylight at 9pm. John took us back to the hotel and said he would pick us up at 7am.

I put in a wakeup call for 6am - took a shower, shaved, and crawled into bed and in seconds was making lots of z's. The phone rang and I sat up in bed and couldn't remember where in the heck I was. I answered the phone and the clerk said "It's 6am", then I remembered. I dressed and went downstairs to the coffee shop for some bacon and eggs. Soon, the others began to appear and when John arrived at 7am everyone was present and accounted for. We finished eating, checked out, and loaded our gear into John's Suburban and headed for the airport.

The pilot of a large single engine Beaver was waiting for us. It was bright red with black trim and had standard landing gear. We loaded our stuff and boarded the Beaver. The pilot cranked her up and in minutes we were roaring down the runway - and I do mean roaring. That was the loudest plane I ever heard. But they say it is stout and reliable. We took off southbound and flew out over the Gulf of Alaska. The pilot didn't gain much altitude and kept scanning the water. In a few minutes he banked sharply and flew us directly over a pod of whales which were coming to the surface and blowing. I suppose this was part of the show; he probably took every load of passengers out over the water to see the whales blow. Anyway, he soon banked around to the west and pulled the nose up and we climbed to about 10,000 feet and leveled off with the coastline off the right wing tip. In a bit we crossed the coast and were over land. Now and then the pilot would point out animals below - bears, caribou, deer, moose, etc.

CHAPTER 4

LAKE ILIAMNA

We had been flying about an hour and a half when the pilot started a shallow bank to the right. As near as I could tell we were now headed north. Within 30 minutes we were over water again and the pilot told us we were over Lake Iliamna and would be landing on the north shore of the lake. He made a call on the radio and started his descent and banked again toward the west. I could see the landing strip ahead. The pilot made a silky smooth landing and we taxied up to a weather beaten building located about midway with the strip. The pilot parked, opened the door, dropped the ladder, and we climbed down - one by one. As the pilot was handing down our gear a man came out of the building and yelled up to the pilot. The pilot dropped a mail sack to him and he went back inside. The pilot soon had everything unloaded and instructed us to stack our gear by the wall, which we did. We went inside and the pilot introduced us to the owner of the general store, a Mr. Teague. The radio crackled while we were talking to Mr. Teague and it was the planes which were on their way to pick us up --they were about 50 miles out and dodging some weather but said they would be landing in about 15 minutes.

We got a cup of coffee and wandered around the store for a few minutes. Then we went outside and saw a small float plane tied up at the dock We walked down to take a look at it. While we were examining the plane, a Cessna, we heard a woman scream and looked in the direction of the scream and saw a man and woman running toward the store as fast as their legs would carry them and following close behind was one huge bear. Mr. Teague must have heard them for he came out the door armed with a rifle. He started toward them and when he reached them he fired the rifle in the air and the bear stopped. He fired once more and dirt kicked up in front of the bear who took the hint and ran the other direction.

When the two victims got their breath they explained they had seen the bears from the air and landed to take some pictures of them. However, they said they got too close to a small cuddly one and the big one started chasing them. Mr. Teague was muttering under his breath as they talked - something about dumb tourist. The couple went on to explain they were newlyweds and were in fact on their honeymoon. They were from Los Angeles and he was a bit player in the movies and she was a school teacher. He was a macho pilot and the plane was borrowed from a friend in Fairbanks. Mr. Teague explained that the bears were raiding his garbage heap and they had encountered an old sow bear with a cub - the worse kind of encounter with a bear. He told them not to do it again. They assured him they would not and immediately got in their plane and took off.

As we watched them climb from the lake we saw a couple of dots to the north that were getting bigger- soon we could hear their engines and tell they too were planes - our rides to Lake Clark. Mr. Teague gave us a lecture about bears *as* we awaited the arrival of our transportation. He said if you left them alone and did not get too close to them they would leave you alone. However, he said hardly a year passes that some damn fool tourist didn't get killed by bears. Matter of fact, he said, about four years ago a man was killed in the same spot the current tourist had their encounter. He even showed us a big sign by the path to the garbage pit that said STAY THE HELL AWAY FROM THE BEARS. He said the bears would sometimes come right up to the door of his store despite the fact that he had a team of sled dogs chained out back. He really didn't like to shoot the bears but had done it a couple of times when he felt he was in real danger. He always kept his 30-06 loaded and handy.

While Mr. Teague was talking the two float planes buzzed the store and swung back over the lake and landed and taxied up to the dock and parked. We helped tie them up and the pilots climbed out and introduced themselves. Both were very young. One was Steve Elmore from Tacoma, Washington. He was a junior at the University of Washington, majoring in Forestry. Steve was a tall, slender blond headed kid with a quick and pleasant smile. The other pilot was an opposite. He was a short, muscular, shy, black headed kid from Duluth, Minnesota. His name was Craig Richards and he was a senior at Marquette University majoring in Sociology. These two young men were going to be our fishing guides and pilots for the next ten days. The Cessna float planes which we would be flying were six place so we would split into groups of five - four of us plus the pilot guide.

CHAPTER 5

LAKE CLARK LODGE

We loaded our gear into the planes for the ride to Lake Clark Lodge which would be our home base for the next ten days. John, Tom, Wallace, and I climbed into Steve's plane and Dewey, Eddie, Don, and Roy climbed into Craig's plane. We kept this pairing for the rest of the trip - it just happened naturally without any conversation or argument. Except for Don and John, we were all very large men (200 pounders plus) and each plane was near its maximum carrying capacity. It was a good thing that Lake Iliama was a large lake because the pilots used up a long stretch of water on the take off. They had to rock the planes on the pontoons to break them loose from the water and get airborne. I looked at my watch; it was 2:30 pm (Sunday). I sat in the co-pilot seat next to Steve. Steve said we wouldn't begin fishing until tomorrow and if we wanted to he would take us on an aerial sightseeing tour of the area on the flight to Lake Clark. We all voted "yes" to that proposition. He called Craig on the radio and told him of our plans - Craig said he would follow. Next, he called Lake Clark and gave them a rundown of the route he would be taking. "Just in case" he explained to us.

For the next two hours we flew over and between mountains and saw glaciers, streams, lakes and many animals including caribou, bears, sheep, wolves plus jillions of fish. We were at a low altitude and the water was so clear that you could see millions of fish in the streams particularly. Steve explained that most of them were salmon who were migrating upstream to spawn. Somewhere along the way in our conversation it came out that I was an ex Air Force flyer so Steve said "You fly for awhile" and gave me the controls. Now and then he would point to a tree, mountain, or other landmark and tell me to fly toward it. It was a terrific experience and I *was* rapidly falling in love with Alaska. After a couple of hours of sightseeing we started crossing over a large lake which Steve said was Lake Clark. He pointed out the lodge over on the east shoreline. We flew over the lodge and buzzed it before turning back over the lake for the landing. When we taxied up to the dock, the entire staff of Lake Clark Lodge lined up to meet us. One held a sign that said "Welcome Texans". That was nice and we were all proud we were wearing cowboy boots. We tied up to the dock and unloaded our gear. The staff helped us carry it to our sleeping quarters - very small two man cabins away from the main lodge. Each cabin contained two beds and two small tables - that's it. There were ten cabins. My roomy turned out to be Wallace - we had become good friends.

After we unpacked we all went to the lodge - and it was magnificent. It was an A frame pattern constructed from native spruce. The front, which faced the lake, was all glass and the view of the lake was breath taking. The lodge was on a small hill and stood perhaps 40 feet above the water level. There was a huge stone fireplace in one end of the lodge and a friendly fire was crackling in it. The kitchen and store room was at the back of the lodge and the bedrooms for the staff were upstairs which was a sort of mezzanine level over the kitchen only. The walls were covered with trophy fish and animals. The tables and chairs were handmade and varnished. I can't describe how beautiful the place was.

We were served cocktails and the cook had prepared a large assortment of hors d' oeuvres which was the start of a culinary delight that lasted throughout our stay. Each of the staff came around and met and visited with each of us. I'm writing this from an old poor memory so if I leave anyone out - forgive me. The staff consisted of Mrs. Swenson, a matronly older lady who served as the cook and chaperone; Jeff, a local Intuit Indian who was the camp handyman, and three teen age young ladies from the University of Wisconsin who served as waitresses, housekeepers, and assistant cooks. These young ladies were Mona, a dark haired and slightly plump young lady who was always happy and laughing; Olga, a blond haired beauty of obvious Scandinavian lineage;

and Mary Jo, another dark headed cutie with a very pleasant personality. In talking to them I learned that all three were college seniors and this was their third summer spent working at Lake Clark Lodge. They claimed they earned much more up here in the wilderness than they could have earned in Wisconsin. The pilots had told me the same thing.

By the time we had pretty much cleaned out all of the chips, dip, pate, smoked salmon, and some kind of meat cut up into small chunks it was time for supper. It was sort of amusing to watch Don and John try to flirt with Olga. First Don would have her attention and tell her some tall tale about Texas only to be outdone by John who would tell some wild story about working on the big pipeline. Obviously she was more interested in Alaska (and John for that matter - John was much younger and closer to her age - and more handsome). I also glanced at Craig who was scowling - apparently he too had some interest in the Scandinavian beauty. Wallace was getting very friendly with Mona and Dewey was talking to Mrs. Swensen. Roy joined me and Tom wandered over. I commented on the large quantity of food they were now beginning to bring to the tables. Steve overhead me and joined us. He explained that nine more guests would soon arrive. He had hardly gotten these words out when the radio crackled and a voice came over the air" Lake Clark - this is Cessna Alpha Foxtrot Niner two - come in" Steve walked over to the radio, picked up the mike and responded. In moments a plane buzzed the lodge, circled back over the lake and landed and taxied toward the docks. We went outside and Steve commented "That looks like a new plane". It literally glistened in the sunlight. Even though the sun was bright, it wasn't real warm outside, probably about 50 degrees. I wished for a sweater or light jacket. We went back inside to the comfort of the fire but everyone else came outside and headed to the docks to meet the new arrivals.

After the new arrivals got settled into their sleeping quarters they came marching into the lodge. We were awed by these folks from Germany. The leader was a short stocky yet distinguished looking man dressed as if he were on safari in Africa He introduced himself as Baron Von Stutts. His traveling companions were Heidi, a blond German beauty who appeared to be his mistress, and his bodyguard, Karl. Karl was a mean looking hombre - he was dressed in a black turtle neck sweater, black trousers, and black boots. He wore a Luger in a holster on his right hip and a long stiletto dagger in a sheath on his left hip. His blond hair was close cropped and he had a mean looking scar that ran diagonally from his forehead , across his eye, and down his left cheek. His grey eyes were mean and scary looking.

Roy visited with the Baron and came back to join us in a few minutes and reported his findings. The Baron was a German industrialist, very wealthy, and his traveling companion, Heidi, was a German movie star (that was certainly believable-she was gorgeous), and his bodyguard had been a high official in the SS Corps (that too was believable). The Baron had come to Alaska to catch king salmon - he had no interest in any other fish or fishing. Throughout the trip the Germans stayed to themselves and spoke only in German. Their private pilot was a famous Alaskan fishing guide named Carl Smith. He too was stand offish and did not mix with any of us or any of the staff of Lake Clark.

We heard two more planes fly overhead and watched them land and taxi to the docks. We began to speculate on the new arrivals. In a while they came into the lodge. Of course, none of us had even come close to guessing as to who or what they would be. Four of them were Japanese business men with enough camera equipment to shoot a Tarzan movie. There was an older retired couple named O'Bryant from New York City. And finally, the last guest was the female editor of a national magazine called THE FLY FISHERMAN. Her name was Betty Scott. The two pilots were also college students who worked for the lodge. Their names were Michael (Mike) and Andrew (Andy). The pilots joined us and we visited awhile. Roy left our group and cornered Ms. Scott. Before he left us he told us that he was a subscriber of her magazine and was going to get her to teach him to be an expert fly fisherman. We found out the following about the latest arrivals. The Japanese were there primarily to take a lot of pictures; the O'Bryant's were there mostly to rest and enjoy the scenery and other guests; and Ms. Scott was there to write an article for her magazine.

Mrs. Swensen asked that we all find a comfortable place to sit so we could watch a film about fishing at Lake Clark. It was a good film and really whetted our appetites for fishing. We were all ready to start fishing immediately but she told us we would be tired of catching fish before our stay was complete. We didn't think that could be possible. After the movie she went over the ground rules of the lodge. Breakfast was served at 6am, dinner at 9pm. Lunch would be a "shore lunch" prepared by the guides. Any time you were hungry, just tell one of the staff and they would take care of your needs. The other rules were simple and basically just good common sense. The main thing was to relax., catch a lot of fish, and enjoy your visit. We would pair up in groups of four and always stay with the guide - no exceptions. (we already knew that). And finally she warned us to force ourselves to get plenty of sleep and rest. She said it would only be dark for about four hours and the temptation would be great to fish too long - especially the first few days.

However, she warned against that and said there were a pair of blinkers on each bed to wear for sleeping - and also be sure to draw the window shades. She said dinner *was* served and *as* soon as we finished eating we should form our groups and select our guides and get together with them next to plan the day's fishing. (This would be a daily ritual).

The dinner she served was fit for a king. It consisted of pot roast with fresh vegetables, a congealed cranberry salad, sour dough bread, and a delicious peach

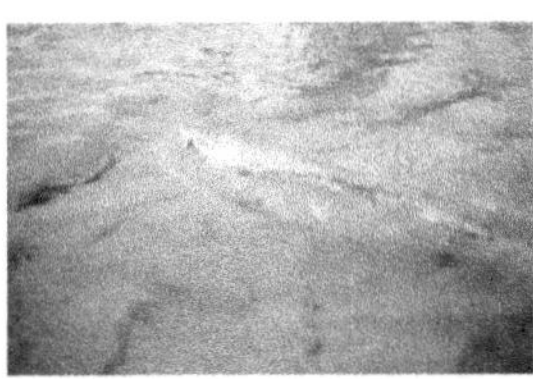

cobbler. By now we were hungry and that made it even tastier. After we ate we had coffee and Steve joined our foursome to plan tomorrow's expedition. Steve unfolded some maps and laid them flat on the table after the girls cleared away the dirty

plates, etc. Steve went over the maps with us and showed us the fishing spots and described the type of fish to be caught in each. Large lake trout in Lake Clark itself(as well *as* several other lakes); king salmon in the Mulchatna river; rainbow trout and greyling in the

Tazmina river; arctic char, salmon, rainbow trout, and dolly varden in the American river; northern pike in Lake Tutna; and "ow heck, any place you see water there is fish of some sort". John piped up and said " Boys, this is a smorgasbord of fishing - the best in the whole world, including Texas). Roy came over to our table and said "Did you boys know that you aren't supposed to use barbed hooks up here?". Why no, we weren't aware of that rule. Steve said "no problem", bring your lures over and Jeff will file the barbs off.

He also said he had a battery powered grinder in the plane and he could remove the barb on a hook in about two seconds - besides, the chance of running into a game warden was very remote (except when fishing for the kings).

CHAPTER 6

KINGS ON THE MULCHATNA

After the delightful supper I poured myself a snifter of cognac, lit a cigarette, and sipped and smoked for a few minutes - until I looked at my watch. It was past midnight and still daylight. This was going to take some getting used to. I went to the cabin, undressed, crawled into bed, put on the blinders and was soon sound asleep. The next thing I knew, Steve *was* shaking me and said "breakfast is ready". I sat up in bed and couldn't figure out where I was - it was pitch black. When I did figure it out, I sheepishly removed the blinders and discovered it was daylight. Wallace was buried under the covers in his bed. I put on my long johns, wool boot socks, wool shirt, blue jeans, and wrestled myself into the waders. (This would be a daily routine, we lived in those waders). I went to the outhouse and took care of biological matters and returned to the cabin and put on a light jacket and my "TEXAN" Stetson before walking down to the lodge for breakfast. I tried to get Wallace out of bed before I left but he threatened me with bodily harm if I didn't leave him alone so I left him alone - he had tested the cognac purty good last night and was a bit overhung.

The food at breakfast *was* also excellent; we were going to gain some weight on this trip if we weren't careful. I ordered sausage, eggs, and pancakes. When the waitress brought the pancakes, she was holding them down. Said they were so light they would float off if she didn't. There was a pitcher of milk on the table. That seemed strange since we were a thousand miles from a supermarket and I hadn't seen a cow since we left Texas. I inquired and was told that a courier plane *came* from Anchorage daily with the mail and the groceries. The waitress further explained that the lodge was famous throughout Alaska for it's fine food. I told her it got my vote for #1.

It took a while but all of our group finally finished breakfast - even Wallace. Steve didn't seem too pleased with our late start and told us to bring the heaviest equipment and lines we had and meet him at the plane ASAP. We asked about lures and he said anything that resembled salmon eggs would work and if we didn't have such - not to worry (He had a plane full of lures we soon discovered). I got my spinning rod and an extra spool of line and a couple of lures and headed for the docks. They were already loading when I walked up and Steve put my stuff in one of the floats and climbed into the plane with me close behind. As would be the standard arrangement, I rode in the co-pilot seat. Steve fired the Cessna up and let it warm up before taxing away from the dock. After Steve signaled, Jeff untied us and shoved us away from the dock and in minutes we were skimming across the water and then into the crisp morning air. Steve took a southeast heading and said we would reach the river in about twenty minutes. He turned the controls over to me and turned around in his seat and told the rest of our group what to expect today - basically a whole bunch of fishermen and some BIG fish.

We were headed toward a mountain and were beginning to get close to it. I asked Steve "Do I go over or around it?" He asked me "What it?" I said "Look for yourself'. He turned around and his eyes got big as he said "Give me the controls" which I did and he banked and headed around the mountain and up a valley. I looked down and saw the river below us. We went around a bend and I said "I don't believe this". Everyone looked and saw the hundreds of float planes tied up to the river bank and further up the river the banks were lined with hundreds, no - thousands, of fishermen. Steve said "Gee whiz, I can't land down there without killing somebody" so he banked sharply to the right and headed back downstream. I said "three aircraft ahead at our altitude - two at eleven o'clock and one at two o'clock" Steve said "Got em, but keep watching". He banked left and started to descend to land. One of the planes from the eleven o'clock position was diving toward the river, obviously trying to land before us. I told Steve what was going on and he said "Air hog - he isn't following proper bush pilot procedures - probably some doctor or something from Anchorage. Having said that, Steve gave it full throttle and went into a much steeper dive toward the river.. We won the race and the other plane pulled up and veered off with Steve giving them the old finger. Even though we landed "hot" it was obvious we were in no danger since we were landing into a rapid current which slowed us down immediately. Steve taxied to the bank and I climbed out and tied us up to a tree.

Everyone climbed out and Steve explained that we would have to walk at least a mile upstream to get past the crowd of fishermen in order to find a section of open bank which we could 'steak out' for our fishing. We said "Fine" and he muttered "That's what you think". He said that we would have to take everything with us and that he would lock the plane. With that he started unloading. He handed us the 30-06 rifle, his camera, the lunch provisions, and all our fishing gear. We were getting ready to head out when John said "Aren't we forgetting something?". Steve said "What?". John responded "The beer". Steve said "It's too heavy, we can drink from the stream". John said "Why can't everyone carry their own?". Steve said "OK" so we each gabbed a few cans and stuffed them in waders, pockets, shirts, etc. and started our journey upstream with Steve in the lead and us strung out single file behind him. We were following a path but the going was tough because of the growth and spongy tundra. We came to a low muddy spot and Steve stopped and we gathered around him as he showed us a huge bear track in the mud. Tom asked "Is that gun loaded?" Steve winked and said "Does the big bear crap in the woods?" and started on down the path (bear path or trail that is).

We started passing the fishermen who were literally shoulder to shoulder on the banks. It looked like a gathering at the United Nations. There were Orientals (many of them), Europeans, Alaskans, and some from the lower forty eight. Most of them waved at us and a few hefted huge king salmon and showed them to us. We saw a few of them fighting fish and heard them yelling and shouting and getting lines tangled. We even saw one fist fight. All in all, it didn't look like my kind of fishing. Steve's either. He explained that when the kings were running, some unscrupulous outfitters put together "one day specials" and hauled the fishermen to this one stretch of the river by the hundreds. He further explained that when the regular guides got there first they would "steak out" *a* stretch of the bank and protect it for their clients. However, since we were running so late, we were left sucking hind tit today. Wallace hung his head momentarily, then opened a beer.

We had walked and stumbled through the brush for over an hour before we finally got past the hoards of fishermen which lined the banks. We continued further upstream although it was tempting to stop and wet a hook Heck , we could see the huge fish in the stream, most were as large as your leg. When the going got too rough we would wade the stream and cross to the other bank. Those river crossings proved the wisdom of wearing waist length waders. The ones with hip length waders got them full of ice water. We came to a fork in the stream and Steve decided this would be our fishing hole for this day. He gathered us around him and explained that we should stay about 50 yards or more apart so we wouldn't get our lines tangled. He helped each of us get rigged up and said if you get a fish on you would have to follow him quite a way down stream before you wore him down enough to land him. He said to watch and listen and if someone upstream of you was coming toward you with a fish on, get your line out of the water and let him pass. (The problem with this was, sometimes when you started reeling in line to get out of the way, the fish wouldn't co operate and you would end up with a fish on your own set. Finally, Steve said that the first people to catch fish should bring them to him - he needed the king to get salmon eggs for bait and we needed a couple of rainbows for lunch.

We all scattered and started looking for our own fishing spot. John and Tom stayed below the fork and Wallace and I each took one of the streams above the fork. As I was moving upstream I kept looking at the fish in the river - there were hundreds of them - all sizes. My guess is that the king salmon ran from about 25 to 70 pounds with an average of possibly 40 pounds. Smaller rainbow trout darted among them, eating the eggs. I finally saw the granddaddy of all , he was much bigger than a second lieutenant. I couldn't stand it any longer so I moved closer to the water's edge and flipped the brilliant pink lure about ten feet upstream of the monster fish. I could see the current moving the lure straight to big daddy. About that time I heard John yell "Fish On". Next, Tom yelled "Fish On". They were a couple of hundred yards downstream from me and I couldn't see them but I was trying to do so. Then I heard Steve yelling instructions to Tom and John. I was so engrossed in listening to what was going on downstream that I had quit watching my lure. A sudden stout tug on my line woke me up. Instinctively, I reared back and set the hook just like I would have done had I been worm fishing for bass back in the Lone Star state. My rod was nearly pulled from my hands and I got a good hold on it and reared back on the rod till it nearly bent double. Line was stripping from the reel so I shifted my position and tightened the drag (some more - it was almost on max. anyway). It felt like I was hooked up with a Mississippi river boat that was moving full steam downstream with the swift current - for a moment anyway- then "PING". The line broke and my first cast became just another "big fish that got away story".

Losing the big fish sort of shook me up so I decided to sit down and have a Marlboro before trying for another king. I examined my rod and it was in good shape and I hadn't lost very much line so I tried on another lure (a red Mepps spinner) and loosened the drag on the reel. I thought a beer would taste good so I popped the top on a beer and sipped on it. The beer was warm so I removed the rest of them and placed them in a shallow spot in the stream and put some large rocks in position so they wouldn't float off in the current. After I finished the beer, I got up and cast the lure upstream and in the deeper water and started to reel it in. A fish hit it on about the third turn of the reel and I set the hook and reeled the fish in - I could tell it was small. When I lifted the fish out of the water it turned out to be a beautiful rainbow trout. I decided to keep the fish as Steve had requested so I added a couple more rocks to my beer storage area and put the fish in there with the beer. Why not catch another trout for lunch I thought so I duplicated my previous cast and caught another rainbow. Now that lunch was taken care of, I decided to get serious about the big boys.

I rummaged around in my small lure box and found another brilliant pink lure similar to the one I had lost and tied it on my line. I could see many kings lazily swimming upstream but none were monster size but I cast the lure out in front of them anyway. Almost immediately there was a tug on the line and I set the hook and stepped into the river and began following the fish downstream. Soon I was almost on top of

John so I yelled "Fish On" and he began reeling in his line and let me pass. I heard someone on the bank yell and looked in that direction and saw Tom holding a large king salmon up and Steve was taking his picture. I continued downstream following the fish and soon Steve was on the bank shouting instructions. I started putting pressure on the fish as he instructed and was able to force the fish on to a sand bar ahead of me. Steve pounced on the fish before it could get back into the current. He lifted the fish out of the water for me to see and released my hook I reeled in my line and waded on down to him. He told me to hold the fish and he would take my picture. He estimated the weight at 35 pounds so I released the fish immediately.

I followed Steve along the path upstream where Tom was waiting. We congratulated each other and Tom said he thought Wallace and John both had fish on- and they did. Before Steve left us to help them he told me to reverse my line on the reel and wait till he returned. Tom said he was going to go catch another big one and as he was leaving I noticed his "lure". I asked "what kind of lure are you using?". He said "Salmon eggs - real eggs". He also said "That's probably why Steve wants you to wait- so he can rig you up with salmon eggs". I sat down and smoked another Marlboro and waited. In a little bit Steve, John, and Wallace walked up.

John *was* dragging a large king-maybe 60 pounds. Wallace said his was bigger but he threw it back - not big enough. He claimed he caught catfish in Tennessee all the time larger than that.

Steve explained that he would rig each of us with salmon eggs and that would improve our chances for a trophy fish. I had already reversed my line and handed my rod to him. He cut off my lure, handed it to me and tied on a treble hook in its stead. Next, he sliced some eggs from a mass of them lying on the ground and sewed them up in a mesh before attaching them to my hook. He examined my reel and took a small screwdriver from his tackle box and tightened the screws in it and pronounced me ready for a big one. Before I headed upstream to my spot I told him about the trout. He said "Great" and explained he would come get them after he got the others rigged up.

When I got to my spot I noted the trout were still there and in good shape. The beer looked tempting so I had another one and a smoke before I cast my eggs to the kings. While I was sitting there I watched several huge fish swim past. I really had mixed emotions about trying to catch one of them. My rod , reel, and line were too lightweight for the huge fish. I couldn't resist and cast the salmon eggs out in the middle of the stream. I wished that I had brought a heavy casting outfit with me. I had originally packed one but let Dewey talk me out of bringing it. Too late to worry about it now, something big had nearly jerked my rod out of my hands and I was tied into a BIG fish now. Same routine, the fish pulled me downstream and there was no way in hell to slow him down. All I could do was hold on and yell "Fish On" and follow him down the river. When I got to the area that John and Tom were fishing a large audience had gathered and was shouting encouragement. The rest of our Texas crew was there along with the Germans. I decided to try the ole sandbar strategy with this fish and started putting *as* much pressure as I dared on him and started wading toward the shore to force him to beach on the sand. Steve saw what I was doing and he headed for the sandbar. To my surprise, it worked again. Steve was able to straddle the huge fish and get his gloved hands behind the gill plates and drag him out of the water. I reeled on down to him and removed the hook. But when I looked at the fish, I was sick. There were large chunks of meal missing from it. Steve explained that the fish had already spawned and was starting to die. He estimated the fish to be about 65 pounds but said if I had caught it a week sooner it would have been a 70 pound trophy fish. Anyway, we drug the fish out onto the bank and everyone came to examine it and take pictures of it. We tried to conceal the white spots where the chunks were missing.

While we were standing around visiting, taking pictures, etc. Steve asked "Anyone getting hungry?" Of course we all were, it was almost 2 pm. He told the new arrivals they would have to catch a couple of trout if they expected to eat with us. Roy had brought a fly rod so he immediately volunteered to catch the trout. I told Steve I would go get the trout I had caught and he said "Try to catch a couple more if you can" and winked. I tied the spoon and hurried back to my spot I caught three more trout in a few minutes and cut a small tree limb for a stringer and headed back downstream with five trout and a couple of cold beers. When I got back to the crowd, Steve had the fire going. I handed him the fish and he and Craig cleaned them in a second. I watched as they placed the trout on aluminum foil and sliced a lemon and placed the slices along each fish. Next, they added slivers of margarine and salted and peppered them before wrapping them in the foil. They scooped away a spot in the coals and laid the fish in it and put coals on top of the packets. Craig opened a couple of large cans of pork & beans and set them on the coals. While he was doing this, Steve was peeling and slicing a couple of large onions and slicing dill pickles. They got out the paper plates and plastic spoons and a loaf of whole wheat bread and yelled "Lunch time". They had to ration the trout and in no time it was gone. Tom asked 'Where is

Roy?". We looked upstream and saw him - He had climbed out on the bank and was trying to dislodge his fly from a tree limb. Dewey yelled "Come on Roy or you are going to miss lunch". Roy joined us and said" I thought they said they needed more trout". Dewey drawled "We do - did you catch any". Roy then began his story about the big one that got away. Meantime, Craig had slipped downstream and caught two more nice trout and he cleaned them and put them on the fire while we hurrahed Roy. Steve put another can of beans on the fire and a can of cream style corn. Craig went back to catch a couple more fish, which he did in short order and added them to the fire. Roy filled his plate and everyone else got "seconds". Steve also put on a pot of coffee. The meal was delicious and the coffee and cigarette afterward was perfect.

We visited some more after lunch and learned that the stragglers had gotten an even later start than us and had stopped and fished with the hoards of fishermen. They had not caught a fish and finally listened to Craig, their guide, and came on upstream. Steve asked us if we would mind if they joined us and fished the afternoon in our staked out waters. We said "OK" but weren't all that enthusiastic - why couldn't they go further upstream? To his credit, Carl Smith, the guide for the Germans , declined the offer and they marched off upstream. We weren't saddened by their departure.

I picked up my rod and started back upstream to my spot. Dewey said he might wander up my way after a bit. My thoughts about the nice Germans was about to charge. When I got to my private spot the Germans had already jumped my claim and Karl had even taken a can or my beer. I walked up to them and explained they were in my territory. The Baron offered to pay me if I would let them stay and Karl just glared at me. I glared back and politely told them to get the heck out of there and stepped out into the stream and cast my lure, which was back to salmon eggs, out into the stream. In less than a minute I had a fish on, and I could tell it was a pretty good one. The Baron was going bananas on the bank and I knew he desperately wanted to catch a king so I motioned for him to come here. He jumped into that river like a Labrador and was at my side in an instant. I handed him my rod and started giving him instructions; don't put too much pressure on the fish, follow him downstream, how we would land him on the sandbar, etc. Carl Smith had joined us and was giving him instructions and encouragement in the other ear and the babe and Gestapo were following us along the bank. The Baron was listening to me only and told Smith to shut up. I yelled "Fish On" as we approached the others and soon we were coming up on my sandbar landing site. The Baron did exactly as I instructed and soon had a 50 pound king beached. I sloshed over to the bank and ran down to the fish and jumped on him. I almost stuck my hand in his gill plate but remembered my gloves just in the nick of time and put them on before I grabbed him and drug him to shore. The Baron waded up and he was grinning like a possum eating persimmons. He was thanking me in both broken English and German. He was one happy camper. Before I could react he stuffed a hundred dollar bill in my pocket I gave it back to him and told him I didn't let him land the fish for money. He asked why I did it. I said, "if you don't know, I can't explain it". To me it was simple common fishing courtesy.

The Baron gave me his business card and invited inc to West Germany as his guest. I told him the next time I *was* in West Germany I would look him up. Since the Baron wanted to keep the fish, Smith rigged up a stringer and tied the big fish to a tree and convinced the Germans to move further upstream. I put more salmon eggs on my hook, borrowed Steve's screw driver and tightened my reel, changed my fishing line, and headed back to my spot By now, I wasn't that enthused about catching any more fish so I had another beer and Marlboro. I could hear "fish on" every so often so I knew some of our group was still catching fish.

I looked at my watch and it was almost 7 so I halfheartedly threw the eggs out into the river and really hoped nothing would bother them. As usual, in just a couple of minutes I was hooked up with another nice king. I followed him down to the sandbar and beached him. I threw my rod over on the bank, put on my gloves, and was dragging the fish to the bank when Dewey walked up. He asked "What are you going to do with that fish?" I said "Throw him back in of course". He said "The heck you are, I want that fish, it will weigh at least forty pounds and I want to have it mounted". I said "He's all yours partner, come and get him". I picked up my rod and headed back upstream. Steve had built up the fire and made a pot of coffee so I stopped and got a cup of coffee and asked how much longer we were going to stay. He said "We always quit at 8 pm". I said "Good, I'm finished for the day". I removed the treble hook and gave it back to him and tightened my poor reel one more time - it had taken quite a pounding. I stayed by the fire until we were ready to leave.

At eight Steve had rounded our crew up and we headed downstream to the plane. We made better time going back because we had nothing to carry except our rods. I was sure glad when we got to the plane and everyone climbed aboard. I helped Steve stow the fishing gear and held onto a pontoon while he cranked her up. After the engine warmed up he signaled for me to shove us away from the bank and climb aboard, which I did. He moved on out to the middle of the stream and took off upstream. About half the planes had already left.

On the flight back to Lake Clark Steve asked me "How did you like fishing for the king salmon?". I said "It was ok, but honestly, I would rather catch black bass back in Texas than fish for those dying monsters. And, I added, there were too dadgum many fisherman in such a cramped up space". Steve smiled and said "You sound like a guide, we don't like to mess with them either". He added, "The balance of your trip will be much more fun".

We landed at Lake Clark without fanfare and dinner was waiting for us when we got to the lodge. The menu tonight was lamb chops and mint jelly. Mrs. Swensen came to our table and apologized for the lamb; someone had told her that Texans hated lamb. We assured her that the lamb was excellent and we were so hungry we would eat anything. The chocolate cake and peaches capped off another excellent meal.

Our planning meeting was short. We decided to give the American River a try the next day. Steve said we would catch very nice trout and arctic char. We went to the cabin and directly to bed, blinders and all.

CHAPTER 7

THE AMERICAN RIVER - CHAR & TROUT

The next morning one of the girls came by and woke us. We got dressed and went to breakfast. As usual the food was excellent. We got our gear (fly rods and spinning rods both for this trip) and met at the dock. Steve was waiting for us and we loaded and were airborne without fanfare. We learned from the day before that Steve didn't like to mess around - he liked to get to the fishing hole early. After we had climbed to about a thousand feet we leveled off and Steve told us this trip would take about an hour and we would be flying over some gorgeous country and would see a lot of game. He asked me to drive and gave me a heading and landmark , then he pulled out a big thermos of coffee and some Styrofoam cups and served coffee to all. Next, he pulled out a sack of fresh made doughnuts and passed them around. Wallace was particularly pleased because he got up late and missed breakfast. About thirty minutes out Steve poked me on the arm and pointed out some moose ahead and to our left slightly. I nosed over into a shallow dive and banked left and made a slow low level circle over them so we could get a good look then climbed back up and continued south. Steve commented to the group "We've got ole Steve Canyon driving this morning." He told me to alter our heading about 20 degrees left and in about thirty minutes we came to a rather large river that looked like a snake; it was really crooked. Steve took the controls and started following the river; looking for a place to land. In a few minutes we came to a reasonably long straight stretch so he banked around and lined up for a landing. As we glided down toward the water he asked "Want to try a landing?"'. "Why not" was my response as I took the controls and did my first landing on floats. It was fun and not that different from landing on a runway.

Steve took over and converted the plane to a speed boat and we raced upstream, skidding around about ten curves in the river until we reached the spot he had selected for today's fishing. That was some ride. He eased the plane gently to the bank and I got out and tied us up to a tree growing on the bank. Everyone climbed out and Steve got our gear from the storage in the floats. We rigged up on the bank as he instructed; shiny spoons on spinning rods and a fly called a scaup (I think) on the fly rods. Then we followed him as he entered the river and started wading upstream. We spread out and began fishing. I had my spinning rod for the start; everyone except John was using spinning tackle. We literally caught a fish on every cast - and it usually was a different kind on the next cast. The first fish I landed was a dolly varden trout, the next was an arctic char, and the next was a rainbow trout. Steve kept a couple of char for our lunch and we released everything else. Each time I took a smoke break, I watched the others catch fish. I had never seen that many fish caught before in my life, and I had been fishing a long time. The only thing I could remember that even came close was fishing for schooling bass - but even then you didn't get a fish every time you cast. This was absolutely unbelievable. After a couple of hours it was getting boring. I told Steve I was going back to the plane and switch to my fly rod and explore downstream a ways. He said "OK, but watch out for bears and be back at the plane by 1 pm for lunch."

We weren't far from the plane. You couldn't see it because it was around a bend in the river. I stayed in the water and waded to it. When I reached the plane I stowed my spinning rod and got my fly rod - and a beer (the beer was kept in the floats and the water temperature was low enough that it stayed cold without ice). I sat on the float with my legs over the side in the water just enjoying the peace and solitude of this beautiful remote wilderness. The water was so clear that now and then I could see a fish leisurely swim past. I flipped the fly out into the current and was sipping the beer when a nice dolly varden tried to run off with my fly rod. I managed to grab it before it hit the water and just let the fish play itself out while I finished my beer. I landed the fish and released it.

A biological urge struck me so I climbed into the plane and located a roll of toilet tissue, unrolled a handful of it and climbed out on the bank. I went downstream a ways and found a small clearing and dropped my waders and jeans and shorts and squatted. About a million mosquitoes attacked my exposed rear. What a predicament and what a terrible choice I was forced to make - mess in my pants or get my rear eaten off by the pesky mosquito's. While I fumbled around in my pockets looking for the mosquito repellent I happened to look at the ground and saw a huge bear track That was all I needed at the moment - a bear. I finally located the repellent and put a generous dose of it on my bare bottom and was able to finish my business in reasonable comfort. I went back to the plane and got my fly rod and decided to do a little exploring downstream. I waded around a curve and could no longer see the plane when I made my first official cast with my fly rod. Almost immediately I had a nice fish on and I fought him into submission and landed him. It was a beautiful arctic char - the largest I had caught or had seen caught. I was tempted to keep him for mounting but without Steve's presence to tell me if he was a trophy or not , I released him. (Later, when I saw the trophy char that Tom kept I realized I had released a real trophy fish- mine was much larger than the one Tom kept - se la viev).

I cast the fly out into the current and got another hit instantly. I was fighting another char almost as large as the one I had just released and had him close enough to get a good look at him when CRACKLE! CRASH! SPLASH! SPLASH! I turned toward the noise and saw a huge bear splashing toward me and my fish. I did what any red blooded outdoorsman would do under the circumstances - I moved as fast as I could toward the plane. I was scared silly and it felt like the river had turned to molasses - I wasn't moving very fast in those waders. I felt a tug on my fly rod and it nearly bent double. I glanced over my shoulder and saw that the bear had caught my char and was stopped and watching me. I certainly wasn't going to argue with him over a little ole fish so I fumbled around and got my knife and cut the line and hustled on to the protection of the plane. When I reached the plane I was shaking so I got another beer to settle my nerves and lit up a cigarette and climbed up on the float. I checked to make sure the plane was not locked (it wasn't) before I sat down on the float to sip beer and smoke.

I was just getting back to normal when I heard SPLASH,SPLASH, SPLASH - and almost went into shock. However, this time the noise was coming from the other direction and when I looked upstream I saw Wallace approaching. He waded up to the plane and I handed him a beer. He joined me on my perch on the float and we sipped on beer and visited. I told him of my experience with the mosquito's and he thought it was extremely funny. (So did everyone else at the lodge later as he told the story over and over). He laughed so much that I decided not to tell him of my other "experience". When he asked if I had caught any fish I told him about the very large char I had landed downstream. He said Tom had caught a trophy sized char and was going to have it mounted. I asked "How big was it?" and he held out his hands to indicate the length of Tom's fish. I said "Mine was at least four inches longer". With that he slid off the float into the water and said "Hot dog, I'm going downstream and see if I can catch him again - and waded off. Soon he was around the bend and out of sight.

I slid off the float and decided to fish near the plane until after lunch. I cast out into the current and had a fish on when I heard Steve, Tom, and John sloshing toward me from upstream. Before they came into view there was a blood curdling scream followed by BEAR! BEAR! HELP! HELP! coming from downstream. All I could hear for the next few seconds was loud splashing in the water as the group from upstream raced toward the plane and pore ole Wallace was trying to get away from the big bear downstream. Steve got there first and grabbed the 30-06 from the plane and headed toward Wallace. Wallace appeared coming around the bend downstream and the bear was nowhere in sight. Steve met him and they both waded back to the plane. When I waded over to the plane Wallace glared at me and said "Why the devil didn't you tell me there was a bear downstream?". I calmly replied 'You didn't ask".

It was lunch time so we all pitched in to help Steve get a fire going and prepare lunch. It was a good thing that an ample supply of firewood was close by - you could not have enticed any of us to venture out into the brush at that time- rifle or no. Shore lunch was delicious. The char was even better than the trout had been the day before. And we even had a big blueberry pie for dessert.

After lunch, Steve decided to move further upstream to another fishin hole. (But I suspect the move was mostly to get away from the big bear, we hadn't begun to fish this place out yet). We loaded our stuff and climbed aboard the plane speed boat and took another exciting boat ride upstream. As we rounded the second bend in the river we almost crashed into three bears who were also "fishing" in the river. They went crashing into the brush as we zipped past. We went around three more bends in the river before we stopped and pulled over to the bank and I hopped out and tied up to a small tree.

We unloaded and started fishing but the fishing wasn't quite as good as the earlier fishing had been. Heck, you sometimes had to cast <u>twice</u> before you hooked a fish. Wallace caught a real nice rainbow trout which he saved for mounting. We continued to catch a variety of fish and John, who had become our unofficial photographer, must have used twenty rolls of film this day. He got some great pictures too. His only regret was not getting a picture of me when the mosquito's attacked - or of Wallace being chased by the bear.

By late afternoon (around 5) it started getting real cloudy and Steve suggested we head on back toward Lake Clark before we got weathered in. None of us wanted to sleep with the bears or spend the night sitting in the plane so we readily agreed to leave. Besides, we were fished out anyway. We loaded our gear once more and climbed into the plane. Steve cranked up and I untied us and shoved the plane away from the bank and took my co pilot seat. We moved out into the middle of the river and Steve pointed her upstream and advanced the throttle. He looked over at me and said "Want to try a takeoff". I looked out and saw we only had about ten feet of clearance between the wing and the bank which was zipping by in a blur and saw nothing ahead but another curve and I finally replied "Heck no- do you think I'm Crazy". Nobody could take off from a snakes back - except Steve. I don't know any pilots who would have even considered a take-off from a winding river like we were on except for this young Alaskan "bush pilot". It was right sportin. After we had gone around the third bend in the river he had enough airspeed to yank the plane into the air and we just barely cleared the trees on the bank ahead of us. I would not have believed such a feat were possible, except I was there and the real Steve Canyon was at the controls.

Once we got into the air I breathed a sigh of relief then looked out - and got scared again. The cloud base was down to about 700 feet and I remembered that we had flown around several mountains on the trip down that were over 1000 feet tall. Steve got on the radio and talked to Iliamna - I could hear his side of the conversation and it did not sound good. The weather was rapidly deteriorating. Steve could see the concern on my face and he said "As long *as* we can see the ground we're ok" . He explained" We'll follow this river and it will take us to Lake Iliamna and from there we'll follow another river up to Lake Clark - No problem". I said "Yeah, right". The guys in the back seat were real quiet.

In about twenty minutes we crossed over a large body of water - Lake Iliamna. We flew across the lake to another river that snaked northward. Where that river emptied into the lake I could see huge schools of fish. I pointed to them and asked Steve what they were. He banked and dived down for a closer look and announced

"Sockeye Salmon", then turned north again and climbed up to about 500 feet. He said "We could come back tomorrow and get after those sockeyes if you all want to". John said "Sounds good but first let's get back to camp". Steve winked at me and replied "No sweat, I've got ole Steve Canyon himself riding shotgun today". We continued north up the river.

The further north we went, the lower the cloud base got. I was beginning to wonder if we were getting into the proverbial position of "Up the creek without a paddle". The base was down to 100 feet or less and we were almost hitting the tree tops. We started going in and out of clouds and finally were in solid clouds. Steve advanced the throttle and pulled the nose up and we started to climb and topped out over the clouds at 6,800 feet. I looked at my watch and at the heading. It was 6:22 and we were on a heading of 5 degrees. I asked Steve if he had a chart in the plane and he asked John to hand him a briefcase in the back of the plane. He opened it and handed me the map. I did some eyeball dead reckoning using mental arithmetic. I figured we would cross over water at Lake Clark at approximately 7:15 - assuming there was no wind. The navigator's mystery is always the wind. Steve's 5 degree

heading assumed no wind and properly so. While we were in sight of land I did not see any signs of wind (i.e. trees swaying, whitecaps on the lake, etc. and Steve said Iliamna reported wind out of the south at 5mph-tail wind with no effect on the heading. We continued north and all we could see were the tops of the clouds and an occasional mountain peak. At ten past seven Steve started his descent and told me we would break out over Lake Clark. I told him I disagreed with him, I believed when we broke out the lake would be a few miles in front of us. He smiled and continued descending...5,000: 4,000; 3,000; 2,000; 1,000. His smile had faded for we were still in thick crud. I kept one eye on the altimeter and one eye watching ahead and one eye on the compass and one eye watching for the ground below. At 200 feet we saw the lake below at the same time but Steve was the first to yell "Lake Clark below". Everyone let out a sigh of relief. There was a beacon at the lodge and Steve picked it out and flew straight to it and made a straight in landing.

It was a happy bunch that crawled out of that Cessna. We got our gear and took it to our cabins and everyone headed straight to the bar. A stout drink was in order. Mrs. Swensen came out and talked to us. She said she was glad we were back; everyone else had come in an hour before us. We all bragged on Steve's flying skills - and navigation skills too. He had done a terrific job of navigating and I told him so. He claimed he had made the flight from Iliamna to Clark so many times he could do it blindfolded.

Our other bunch (Dewey, Eddie, Don, and Roy) plus two of the Japanese had a hot poker game going. We stood around and watched them for awhile and sipped our drinks. Finally Tom found another deck of cards and tried to get another game started. We told him we would play if he kept it to a 25 cent limit and could find a couple more players. In a minute he came back with Betty and Mr. O'Bryant in tow. We moved a table closer to the fireplace and started a low stakes, friendly poker game (the other game was not low stakes, therefore not too friendly). We were really enjoying ourselves and wondering what the pore folks in Texas might be doing about now. No telling.

We were really enjoying the poker game, no one was winning much and no one was losing much, we were just having fun. Tom looked over at the other table and asked "Who's winning?" Dewey respond "Eddie - who else. He's already won enough money to burn a wet elephant with". Mrs. Swensen appeared and said "Supper is served, and I've fixed a special meal just for you southern boys tonight". We got up and went to the dining table and gazed at the spread before us - fried chicken, mashed potatoes, green beans, cream gravy, and hot biscuits. Yummy, yummy - shut my mouth. It was delicious and she topped it off with peach cobbler and ice cream. Oh well, another 10 pounds and an inch on the waist line.

After we finished we had our usual planning meeting with Steve and agreed to try the sockeye salmon tomorrow. I went to the cabin and went to bed but most of the others, including my roommate, stayed up and played more poker. I awoke the next morning to Mona's voice, she was shaking Wallace and saying "Time to get up honey, breakfast is ready". I pulled off my blinkers and rolled out of bed and dressed. When I headed to the lodge for breakfast, Wallace was still snoring.

CHAPTER 8

SOCKEYES AT LAKE ILIAMNA

Tom, John, and I had finished breakfast and were sipping coffee and smoking while we waited for Wallace. Steve got up from the guide's table and joined us and said Wallace did not want to fish today; he wasn't feeling well. He also asked if we would mind if Betty took his place today. We said "fine". He said our other group was going on a float trip today and the Germans and Japanese were going back to Mulchatna to fish for kings but Betty had said she didn't want to go with them - she wanted to fly fish. He walked over to the table where Betty was sitting and told her then returned and said we would depart in ten minutes.

I excused myself and headed for the library for a morning constitutional - I didn't want the mosquito's gnawing on my tail today. I finished my job and went by the cabin and got my gear and headed for the docks. Everyone was loading and waiting for me and Betty, who got there in a couple of minutes. Steve cranked up and I shoved us away from the dock and climbed aboard. Steve told me to take off so I glanced out and looked at the wind sock. I taxied out into the lake and pointed her upwind and shoved the throttle forward. We went skimming across the lake and when the airspeed reached 125 I rocked her a couple of times and broke the suction on the pontoons and we jumped into the air. I banked around to a heading of 185 degrees and climbed up to a thousand feet.

In about 30 minutes I could see Lake Iliamna ahead but I had gotten off course a little - the river joined the lake ahead and on our right slightly so I banked right and corrected and when we crossed over the lake I let down and landed so we would coast to the bank to the right side of the mouth of the river. When we flew over we saw that the fish were still there, millions of them. When we nudged up to the bank I shut her off and noticed there were no trees to tie up to. I asked Steve if we should move. He said "No" and we unloaded. Steve got a metal stake out of a pontoon and drove it into the bare bank and tied us up. He told us the lake got deep not far from shore and suggested we fish the river, which was shallow, or from the bank.

Betty marched off toward the river and we followed along behind. She waded out and started casting with her expensive split bamboo fly rod. We stood and watched her for awhile - she was good. After we watched her catch a couple of sockeyes, we started fishing. Although I could cast the fly and catch fish on my cheap plastic fly rod, I was not in the same league as Betty.

As usual, we caught fish on practically every cast and as usual I got bored by mid morning. I finally got up the nerve to ask Betty if she would give me some lessons in fly fishing. She said "Sure". She told me lesson number one was "Get good equipment before you begin" (I had noticed her eying my cheap outfit). She handed me her rod and said "Try this".. The rod was light as a feather and I whipped the fly out and back a few times before I let it settle on the water. I felt a tug instantly and set the hook and fought the fish and landed it. Fishing was a lot more fun with this expensive rig. I gave the rod back to Betty and asked what lesson number two was. She said" You're pulling my leg cowboy, you don't need lessons - all you need is good equipment, let's go back to the plane". I followed her back to the plane and she got her spare rod out of the pontoon and rigged it for me. We went back to the river and I had a ball catching fish on this feather light equipment. John, as usual took several more rolls of pictures and promised Betty he would send her some copies.

Steve finally yelled "Lunch time" and we gathered back at the plane. He said "How would you like to try something different for lunch?". We asked what he had in mind and he replied "Moose burgers". We said "Why not". So we climbed back into the plane and Steve cranked up and we taxied down the lake to the docks at Teague's general store. We tied up and walked toward the store. Mr. Teague was outside, bending over a grill, and as we got closer could smell the meat cooking. (Steve had called him on the radio and ordered the burgers).

We went inside and got cokes and chips and back outside where Mr. Teague served up "genuine Alaskan moose burgers". He had seasoned them with dehydrated onion soup and they were delicious - another gastronomical treat in Alaska. While we ate Mr. Teague entertained us with his wild stories about living in the wilds of Alaska - he had lived here for 33 years.

After lunch Steve asked "What do you want to do this afternoon?". Betty was the first to speak up and she of course wanted to do more fly fishing - particularly for trout. Tom suggested more sightseeing. Steve then suggested we go sightseeing for an hour or so and then go back to the American river and fish some. We thought he just wanted to scare Betty with another zig zag take off and we had not forgotten how scared we were yesterday so we weren't that thrilled with his suggestion, and told him so. Steve promised he would take off from the straight stretch and we finally agreed. HE LIED.

Steve refueled the plane before we climbed aboard. Soon we were back in the air, lazily flying up valleys teeming with game - moose, caribou, wolves, bear, etc. We flew over a glacier that was massive but by now this was getting to be old hat - but a gorgeous old hat it was.

Betty had not been on an aerial tour and she took tons of pictures. She spotted an old sow bear below with a baby and asked Steve to land so she could get some closer pictures of them. The only water below was a small stream and Steve refused. (The kid had more sense than I had given him credit for).

When he headed South I knew we were on our way to the American river. By now I had learned some of the landmarks and lay of the land. After a while we crossed over the American and he turned and headed downstream for the straight stretch. We soon reached it and he flew over it and banked and landed upstream. Then we went on the wild boat ride just like the day before. He finally pulled up to the bank and I got out and tied us to a tree. It was the same spot we had tied up the previous day - our tracks were everywhere - mixed in with fresh bear tracks. When they climbed out Betty exclaimed "How thrilling". (I thought - just wait till we take off- I figured he would pull the same stunt again).

While we were rigging up to fish Betty told me to continue using her spare rod which I gladly did. We all waded out into the stream and started upstream and *as* we rounded the bend Betty (who always jumped out in front) screamed. That old bear was out in the middle of the stream, fishing again. We all yelled at him but he didn't budge - can't say that I blamed him - he was there first. We opted to fish downstream. Soon we were all catching fish -char, rainbows, and dolly vardens. The only difference was they were a lot more fun to catch on the split bamboo I was using today. Betty joined John in taking pictures and asked me to take some of her using her expensive camera - which I did. Time flies when you are having fun and before we knew it the old 7 had rolled around on the watch. Steve said it was time to go. Betty asked me to go upstream with her to get a few pictures of the bear. I politely declined but Steve volunteered. He got the 30-06 and told us they would be back in a few minutes and for us to load up. We watched them slosh upstream and waited. Sure enough, in a few minutes we heard Betty scream and that was followed in a few seconds by a BOOM! John said "They found the bear". Tom said "Wonder if she took any pictures?". Soon they came running down the opposite bank toward us. When they got a beam of the plane they jumped into the river and waded across. We kept watching but the bear didn't appear.

Betty was bug eyed and scared to death and she immediately climbed into the plane an snuggled up in the rear seat. Before we loaded Steve told us what had happened. Betty was taking pictures of the bear and had her eye in the camera and walked toward the old saw. She got too close and the bear charged. He shot in the water just to scare the bear.

We saw the rest of the story. We climbed aboard and I untied us and climbed in. Sure enough, Steve pointed the plane upstream and we all knew what that that meant. He explained it was quicker than the long taxi back to the straight stretch and just as safe. Un huh.

He shoved the throttle forward and we went zipping around corners just as the day before. The only difference was Betty's screams. After the third curve Steve yanked her up and a pontoon actually clipped the lop of a tree as we crossed the bank. I know because a part of a tree limb was on the pontoon when we landed. Except for the scary takeoff, the trip to the lodge was uneventful.

After we landed and put our gear in the cabins I went to the lodge. Wallace and Mona were sitting by the fire and Betty was sitting alone with a stiff drink in her hand. Tom came in and we got ourselves a drink and joined Betty. She was still shook up and said she had never been so frightened in her life. We talked for a while and learned that she was actually the owner and editor of the magazine. She was divorced and lived in Seattle with two teen aged daughters. She traveled all over the world, fishing and writing stories for her magazine. She was a very interesting person and very friendly, once you got to know her.

The rest of the Texas crew showed up and joined us. By now, Betty was more relaxed and told them of today's harrowing experiences. Then Dewey told us all about their day - floating leisurely down the Tazimina river. It sounded like fun. Supper *was* served (ham tonight) and after the meal we held our planning meeting. I suggested we do the float trip and everyone agreed. Steve said he didn't do the float trip but he would check with Craig and see if we could switch. He returned in awhile with Craig and said the switch was ok with everyone. Craig described the float trip and asked that we be at the dock in the morning - equipped with fly rods.

I retired to the cabin and the soft bed- tired and over fished.

CHAPTER 9

FLOATING THE TAZIMINA

The mornings by now were routine and this one was no different, except when we got to the dock. There were two float planes and three pilots (Craig, Mike, and Andy) waiting for us. Craig explained that Mike and Andy

would follow us and bring his plane back to camp. We climbed aboard and in a few minutes were airborne and headed in a northwest direction. About thirty minutes later Craig landed in a small lake and taxied up to shore. We unloaded and watched the other

plane land and they taxied over and joined us. Included in the gear we unloaded were two large bulky packs (obviously the rafts) . The two planes took off and left us - out in the middle of nowhere. We picked up the gear and Craig led off We were following a narrow path and the footing was bad; we took turns carrying and dragging the bulky raft packs.

After an hour of struggling we finally came to the river. The bank was very steep and all loose rocks. Craig tied a rope to a tree and we slid down the bank, one by one, holding on to the rope for dear life. Next, Craig inflated the rafts with gas cartridges, and tied them to the rope and slid them down to us. Finally he came sliding and tumbling down. We launched the rafts and Craig, Tom, and I got into one and John and Wallace the other. The water was clear, cold, and swift, very swift. We only used the paddles to steer, the current did the rest. If you looked down into the clear water you would often see a big fish; if you looked up you often saw an eagle soaring in the bluest sky imaginable, and if you looked toward the shoreline you might see some sort of animal - beaver, mink, otter, big bear, moose. It was absolutely heavenly floating down that Pristene river and enjoying nature.

Occasionally Craig would have us paddle like heck to get to the bank. We would beach the raft and get out - sometimes to fish or sometimes just to stretch our legs. When we fished it was nearly always in the smaller side streams that ran into the river and the fish caught were nearly always trout. The fly which worked best was called a scupper but you could

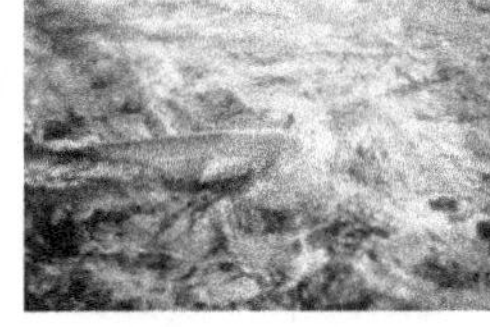

catch fish on anything.

On about our sixth stop, Craig told us the small stream we stopped for was famous for its trophy greyling. He said the world record had been caught in this stream. Wallace asked "What the blazes is a greyling". Craig described them and said if you caught one you would know - it's dorsal fin was almost as large as it's body. You could see the little rascals in the clear water - always on the far bank. We all tried very hard to catch one, but without success. Even Craig couldn't catch one and he kept changing flies on each cast. Everyone gave up on them and returned to the river and caught trout - everyone except me. I was determined to catch a graveling just to see one up close. I followed Craig's method and tied on a different fly for each cast - nothing enticed them. About the only thing in my box I hadn't tried was a very ugly looking bumble bee -yellow, orange, with black circles around its fat little body. Why not. I tied the bumble bee on and flicked it toward the other bank - WHAMO! One of the little devils hit it. That small fish fought as hard, if not harder, than a larger trout. Soon I landed him and yelled for the others to see him. They all rushed over and examined this strange little fish. Since everyone wanted to catch a grayling, I let them take turns using my rod and bumble bee until they

caught one. John caught the largest one and decided to keep him and have him mounted. (Didn't make sense to me - it couldn't have weighed two pounds -fin and all).

At our next stop we had lunch - trout and beans. Craig put on a pot of coffee so we took an extended lunch break We could see some eagle nests across the river in tall trees and we watched eagles swoop down and catch fish and take them back to their nests for the baby eagles. This was a delightful spot and the weather was perfect. John even commented "It's almost warm enough to go swimming". We said "You've been in Alaska too long - you're nuts" With that he jumped up and started stripping and the next thing we knew he jumped in the river. He was splashing around and hooting and hollering - seemed to be having a lot of fun. Why not? We all stripped and joined him. The fun didn't last too long though - the water temperature was about 35 degrees. We were soon back on the bank and building up the fire to thaw out. About that time we heard a loud noise coining up the river, sounded like a jet airplane taking off We watched as a flat bottomed boat came around the bend and headed toward us.

When it went past we saw two Intuit Indians who were holding on the side of the jet powered boat as it raced past. They waved at us and we waved back After they had passed and the noise subsided, Wallace said "Wonder where they are going - and why". Craig said "They are saying - Wonder what those bare assed tenderfeet are doing by the fire - and why" We all laughed and got dressed.

We got back into the rafts and continued downstream, stopping often to fish. I was enjoying the floating and looking as much the fishing. In mid afternoon we went to shore and beached the rafts at the largest feeder creek we had come to. Craig said "This creek has some really nice rainbow trout". John said "Yeah, we know - world record stuff - right?" Craig ignored him. We started up the feeder creek - John and Tom began fishing. Craig stayed with them but Wallace and I continued up the creek. Wallace finally stopped and cast and hooked a fish; I kept moving upstream.

About a hundred yards past Wallace, the creek had a sharp bend in it. The rushing water had cut a cave into the outer bank and there was a tangle of exposed tree roots in the cave. The water was aqua in color - very beautiful and very fishy looking. I went past it and flicked my fly out into the current and let it carry it to the cave. Each time the fly got near the cave a rainbow trout darted out and gabbed it. I caught several and all were in the 5 to 6 pound range. However, I was convinced the world record was hiding in that cave and I was determined to catch him. I finally decided to wrap some lead on my line and try to get the fly further into the cave and deeper and under the roots. I flicked the fly back out into the rapid current and felt it bounce along the bottom and watched as it disappeared into the aqua water and head straight to the cave. I held my breath and in a second felt a solid strike and set the hook No doubt this was a good fish, my rod was bowing pretty good. The fish finally came out of the deep water and headed downstream, stripping line as he went. I started following the fish and when I saw Wallace I yelled "Fish on" (just like the kings). Wallace took his line in and waded to shore and when the fish got near him (by now he had stripped most of my line and I was 60 or 70 yards away) it decided to come out of the water. The giant rainbow came out of the water in an arcing jump, what a beautiful sight Wallace yelled "Hang on Bill, you've got a world record on" He had barely gotten the words out of his mouth when "PING!" - the leader broke. Another big one got away. (Folks, I know that everyone is skeptical of any fisherman's tale about the BIG one that got away - but, in this case, I've got proof. Any time you want to see it I'll show you that broken leader.)

I was so disappointed that I didn't even rig up again. I just went to the raft and smoked while I waited for them to finish (Of course, Wallace told them about the twelve to fifteen pound Rainbow and they were all trying to catch him again). They finally showed up, but none had caught the big trout.

We floated on down the river and made two more stops. At each stop we caught more trout and released them. By now it was getting late in the afternoon. We started on down the river and rounded a bend and saw a large lake ahead. Craig said it was Lake Clark. We paddled on out into the lake and waited. We could see a small village on the bank near where the river emptied into the lake. Craig said it was called Nondalton. It was a few minutes past seven and the planes had not arrived to pick us up. Craig was getting upset so we paddled to the bank near the village and Craig went to a house and borrowed a phone and called the lodge. We took a short tour of the village while we waited for our ride home. We watched some Indians cleaning and drying fish. Craig explained they caught them in traps. We heard our planes coming so we got back into the rafts and paddled out into the lake again - soon two Cessna's taxied up to us and we climbed aboard. Craig deflated the rafts and stowed them and we took off and flew back across the lake to the lodge - about a 5 minute flight. Thus ended one of' the best days of the trip. If I ever return to Alaska to fish, I will certainly include as many float trips as possible.

That night after supper we were having trouble deciding where to fish the next day. By now we were spoiled and I suppose just getting tired of catching fish. Steve kept suggesting places where we would catch more trout - no one was interested. I finally asked "What about pike?'. Steve thought that was a good idea and said "I know a small lake up in the mountains that is loaded with northern pike, but, he added, they aren't very large". We asked "What is large?". Steve explained that further south (in Canada), the pike and muskies grew to the 30 pound class but the ones this far north rarely got over 15 pounds. We said "That's big enough, let's try them" So the agenda for the next day was "NORTHERN PIKE".

CHAPTER 10

NORTHERN PIKE

As we boarded the Cessna the next morning for our pike fishing expedition, I could tell that something was different. Steve kept looking at his watch and did not seem to be in any hurry to take off He finally cranked up the engine but shut it off and climbed out and lifted the cowling and pretended to be checking on something. While he was diddling around we saw Craig and Olga come down the steps, walk down the ramp, and climb aboard Craig's plane. Each of them had been carrying a basket. Strange. Steve immediately got back into the plane and cranked up and in minutes we were skimming across the lake and took off and climbed out. We flew north by northeast for over *an* hour and landed on twin lakes which were connected by a stream and nestled high up in the mountains.

Steve taxied up to the bank and we climbed out and stepped on the bank - Steve had warned us the lake was deep along this bank. We climbed out and jumped from the pontoon to the bank. Steve unloaded our gear and handed it to us. While we were unloading, Craig landed on the lake and taxied over to us. Olga got out and stepped to the bank and Craig handed her the two baskets. We were quite puzzled as to what the dickens was going on and Steve finally gathered us together and said "Olga wanted to come with your group today and cook your lunch, even though it is her day off Craig and I have to fly-to lake Iliamna and pick up another group of fishermen so you will be on your own. I'll leave the rifle, just in case, and we'll be back around 7pm to pick you up." He explained that both lakes were packed with northern pike and only the south shore was shallow, enough to, wade. "Good luck and-good fishing was his parting comment. He and Craig took off end left us all alone - except for Olga. It was a strange feeling, watching the planes disappear on the horizon. What if they don't return-ran through each of our minds.

We were really out in the middle of nowhere and Steve said "No one ever came out here fishing. They would come get us. No sweat. But what was the deal with Olga? We started discussing the situation and none of us had any idea she was coming - none of us old folks that is. John, the bachelor, finally admitted he had sort of suggested it to her the night before. Ah Ha! Now the truth comes out. We had already suspected that John was sort of sweet on Olga - even from day one. But we didn't realize she had her bonnet set for John.

John helped Olga carry the grocery baskets to a grove of trees and, they set up a temporary "camp". John built a fire and she unpacked. We just watched. John finally said "You guys go ahead and fish, I'll stay here and help Olga, besides she is afraid of the bears". We said "So are we". Finally Tom said "Aw heck, let's go fishing". We went down the bank a ways and began fishing. Tom and Wallace had already caught a fish before I was even rigged up. They were using spoons. I decided to try a plastic worm which I found in my tackle box. I flipped it out and felt a vicious strike. I set the hook and reeled in a long, slimy, teeth snapping northern pike - YUK. Whose idea was this? I-used. my pliers to get the ugly devil off my hook. Besides his bad looks, he had destroyed the plastic worm with those sharp teeth. I tied a Johnson silver spoon and followed Tom and Wallace down the bank. Like everywhere else we had fished, the going was tough on the bank and the vampire mosquito's were everywhere. The soil was tundra like, real spongy, and the grass and weeds were thick. We would stop now and then and cast out into the lake and catch a northern pike on every cast. Finally we wandered upon an old abandoned log cabin and stopped to investigate it. It contained many of the "possessions" of the trapper who had abandoned it, many years before. We found steel traps, pots and pans, pelt boards, old books, etc. It was very interesting to see how someone had lived in this wilderness. Tom said "We ought to hang around here and wait till John joins us".

Wallace said "Heck Tom, he ain't going to join us today - he's got something on his mind besides fishing". And he was right, John and Olga spent the day at the makeshift camp - cooking lunch, drinking wine, and whatever.

After we fished on past the cabin about a hundred yards we came to the creek that connected the two lakes. The creek really looked fishy so I cast downstream and started to reel the spoon in when WHAMO - something big hit it and ran upstream and out into the deep water of the lake. I couldn't turn the fish and it almost stripped all my line. He finally turned and headed back toward the creek and I frantically reeled in line. When he got back into the creek I put all the pressure I could on my rod and line and PING - the line broke (or he cut it with his sharp teeth).

Tom and Wallace had been watching and I walked back to where they were and told them my line had snapped. Tom examined it and said "Why weren't you using a wire leader?". I said "Don't have one". He rummaged through his pockets and handed me a wire leader which I tied onto my line and hooked on another spoon. Wallace said "I'm getting hungry' (meaning I'm so curious about what nephew John is up to I can't stand it), but first I've got to water the plants".

Wallace wandered off into the brush and was gone for a few minutes. While Tom and I waited for him we heard a strange noise that sound like bones rattling and a calf bawling - Baaa.... Wallace soon rejoined us and Tom asked "Did you hear a strange noise?" Wallace replied "Yep - seen it too". Tom said "What was it?" Wallace said, " Two of the biggest, meanest, vicious mosquito's you ever saw were setting down on the remains of the skelton of a moose calf they had eaten - one of them was rattlin two bones and the other one was bleating like a calf. Tom asked "Wonder why they were doing that?" Wallace winked at me and replied "Reckon they was trying to call up the mama moose?"

We followed Wallace back to "camp" and when we got there it was deserted. There was a pot of stew and a pot of coffee on the coals - but no John or Olga. Tom yelled and they answered , further down the lake. They soon walked up, clad in bathing suits. They said they had been swimming. Olga was sunburned. She scurried around and soon served each of us a steaming bowl of delicious stew, some homemade rolls, and a cup of wine. Another delicious meal. By now we were tired of fishing so we sat around camp and drank coffee , smoked, and talked for a couple of hours.

We finally decided to fish some more (or at least explore the second lake) so we headed back down the bank. John and Olga followed us; they wanted to see the old trapper's cabin and take pictures of it. We stopped a couple of times and caught fish; and let Olga or Juan reel them in. We got to the cabin and they stopped and we continued to the connecting stream and fished it a few minutes before proceeding to the next lake. We caught several fish in the stream; but no one hooked the big one.

When we got to the second lake there were several beavers swimming in it and when they spotted us the hit the water with their flat tails and disappeared. We continued around the bank and came to the beavering dam; which really was the reason there was a lake. The water was clear and came to a shallow stretch past the dam. We were able to wade out and the going was much easier. We caught dozens of pike and soon my lure was chewed up beyond recognition. I rummaged through my pockets and couldn't find another spinner or spoon. I asked Tom and Wallace if they had any spare lures. Wallace pulled out what he described as a "patriotic spinner bait" and pitched it to me. It was literally a spinner that was red, white, and blue. Wallace said he had received it from Bass Masters when he joined. I hooked it onto my wire leader.

On the first cast my line got tangled and die lure fell about two feet from me in the clear water - I could see it lying on the bottom. It took me a couple of minutes to unsnarl my line and before I began to reel it in I glanced down at the lure. It was surrounded by hungry northern pike - like a bunch of mad Indians circling a wagon train. It was then that I invented a game - keep away. I reeled the line down until I took the slack out of it then lifted the lure out of the water - the pike literally were jumping out of the water - trying to catch it. Next, I cast the lure out and reeled it back as fast as I could and when it was nearly at my feet I would quickly lift it out of the water and watch the pike jump and snap at it. I was actually trying NOT TO CATCH A FISH! Believe it or don't, most of the time I could not succeed - I nearly always hooked a fish.

Tom and Wallace waded over close to me and watched. Wallace asked "What in heck are you doing?'. I explained the game and Tom said "It's time to head back to Texas when the fishing (or non fishing) has sunk to this level." "I really couldn't argue the point, we were all "fished out". We were scheduled to depart day after tomorrow and I was seriously thinking about staying in camp tomorrow myself It was past 6pm so we headed back toward "camp". As we were walking back we heard airplanes in the distance and they had landed and taxied to the bank and John and Olga were loading when we walked up. We climbed aboard and were soon on our way back to the lodge.

P.S. This chapter would not be complete without telling you that Olga and John were married about a month later, So you see, this was a very productive day after all.

CHAPTER 11

LAKE TROUT ON LAKE CLARK

This was our last day of fishing in Alaska. Tomorrow, a twin float Beaver was scheduled to pick us up at 8 a.m. and take us to Anchorage and our commercial flight departed Anchorage at 1 p.m. As I've already explained, we were all about fished out anyway so we were ready to leave.

That morning at breakfast the guides said that the day would be devoted to catching fish to take home with us. They recommended a return trip to Lake Iliamna to load up on the cutthroat salmon. Everyone except me agreed with the suggestion. I had seen a couple of boats with outboard engines tied up at the dock and I inquired if I could use one of them. Steve said "Sure, do you want to fish on Lake Clark - it has big lake trout in it". I said "Why not". Steve replied "Would you mind if Jeff (the Indian handyman) went with your I said "I would be very pleased if he would".

I walked down to the dock and watched everyone crawl aboard the two Cessna's. Before Steve got in he handed me two jigs and said "Try these, they work good on the lake trout". I thanked him and he said that Jeff was getting his gear together and would be down in a few minutes. I waved goodbye as they taxied from the dock.

As the planes were taking off Jeff walked up and said "Ready?'. "Sure" I replied and he started loading his stuff in the boat. I hustled back to the cabin and got my spinning gear and returned; Jeff already had the 35 hp Mercury warmed up so I threw my rod in the boat and stepped in. Jeff backed us away from the dock and asked where I wanted to fish. I said "Wherever the big ones are".. He laughed and pointed the boat toward the north and we ran about 100 yards offshore for perhaps 20 minutes and he dropped the speed to idle and finally put the engine in neutral and said "Big Ones." He cast his lure off

to the left and I tied one of the jigs and cast off to the right. Jeff put the engine in gear and we idled along. It was obvious we were going to troll.

My lure was bumping the bottom so I took up slack until it was floating freely. I noticed that Jeff's lure was also on bottom so I suggested he take in a little line, and he did. He confessed that he hadn't fished much with lures; his strong preference *was* a fish trap. He said he was a meat hunter and fisherman and wanted to keep anything we caught I laid my rod down so I could light up a cigarette.

WHAM - Something hit my lure just as I held my lighter to the cigarette. I dropped the lighter and grabbed for the rod, and missed. Luckily, Jeff (who was in the end of the boat) grabbed it just before it went overboard. He handed it to me and the battle was on - it obviously was a nice fish. in a few minutes I had him up close to the boat and Jeff scooped him up with the large net *in* the boat. It was a beautiful lake trout; probably 30 pounds. Jeff put him on a stringer and I cast out again.

As the lure was sinking I felt a tug on the line and set the hook. I could tell it was another nice fish so I just handed my rod to Jeff and told him to land the fish. He smiled broadly and his eyes gleamed; he had a ball fighting that fish. When he finally got him up close to the boat I got the big net and scooped him up. Jeff was so proud of that fish- said it was the biggest he had caught on a rod.

I lit another cigarette and offered Jeff one, which he accepted. He was still excited from fighting the 30 pound trout. While we were smoking and drifting I had Jeff hand me his rod and I reeled it in and replaced the battered spoon he had tied on with one of the jigs that Steve had given me. I cast both lures out and handed Jeff's rod back to him. I held my rod and every now and then yanked it up and let the jig free fall. Jeff imitated me. Before we could finish smoking we each hooked a fish. I could tell that the fish I had on wasn't as large *as* the first and when I netted him he was about 15 to 20 pounds. Jeff's was slightly larger - but he strung up both.

We sat in that spot and jigged for another hour but didn't catch another fish. I guessed that these fish ran in schools and the school we had caught fish from had moved. I suggested that we too move. Jeff didn't want to move but I finally convinced him. He cranked up the outboard and looked at me and asked "Where to?". It appeared our roles were reversing - I was becoming the guide. What the heck, I was just killing time more than anything else, so I pointed to the north along the shoreline so we ran further up the lake and in about ten minutes I yelled "stop". and he shut off the outboard.

As we dropped the jigs over the side and were getting set to fish, Jeff looked at inc and said "No good place- no big fish here", and it turned out he was right We fished for over an hour and didn't get a strike. I finally suggested that we troll back toward the lodge and Jeff thought that was a good idea so he cranked up the outboard and swung the boat around and we headed south at an idle. We had gone perhaps 300 yards when Jeff's rod bowed and he let out a whoop -- it *was* obviously a large fish. I started to reel in my line as fast as I could and something struck my jig but I missed setting the hook I let the jig float down toward the bottom and felt a tug on it and reared back on the rod and set the hook. I was watching Jeff out of the corner of my eye and he had his hands full with his fish. My fish *was* another small one and I landed it quickly, took the hook out, and dropped it in the bottom of the boat. By now, Jeff had his fish about 20 feet from the boat and I got the landing net and got in position to net the fish when he got it in closer. When he got the fish up close to the boat he yelled and I saw the reason - the fish was huge. I wasn't sure the net was large enough. It wasn't. I put on my gloves and gabbed the fish by the lip with one hand and behind the gill plate with the other and it took all my strength to pull him over the gunnel and into the boat. As I was doing this, Jeff was whooping and hollering. I took the hook out of its mouth and Jeff said "We go" and he cranked up and sped toward camp.

We were the first back to camp but Jeff yelled and hollered so much that all the staff came to the dock to examine our catch. I helped Jeff carry the fish up to the "smoker" where he cleaned them and placed the fish on the racks in the smoker to smoke them for next winters food. Speaking of food, I was starved, it was 4:00pm and we hadn't eaten since breakfast and it was 5 hours till supper. I suggested to Jeff that we go to the lodge and see if *we* could get fed and he liked the idea.

Mrs. Swensen was in the kitchen, roasting a turkey for supper. We told her we were starved so she got a leftover roast out of the refrigerator and warmed it up. We got a loaf of bread and made sandwiches. Jeff got a couple of cokes and we went out on the front porch to eat our late lunch. It was so peaceful and quiet and the scenery was breathtaking. I'll always remember that view from the front porch of Lake Clark lodge; *as* far as I am concerned it is one of the most beautiful spots on the face of the earth. Jeff had chores to do so I just sat on the porch for a couple of hours and rested.

Around six o'clock the planes returned from Lake Iliamna. I walked down to the dock to meet them. They had caught a lot of fish; more than they wanted to carry home. When I told them of the large lake trout we had caught I had to take them to the smoker to "prove it". Dewey said "Anyone want to go lake trout fishing" - but he had no takers and he got upset with me for not taking him out.

We had a turkey and all the trimmings for supper that last night at Lake Clark Lodge. Even though we had caught more fish than we ever dreamed possible these last six days and were burned out on fishing; we were all a little saddened at the thought of leaving in the morning. We had made a lot of new friends and it was obvious we had been something special for them too and I think they hated to see us leave. After supper we were reminiscing about all the wonderful adventures and Wallace jumped up and grabbed a hat and passed it around and said "Dig deep, we're going to leave a big tip for these folks" - and we did. I went to bed but most everyone else stayed up late and partied, or, so I'm told.

The trip back to Texas the next day was uneventful; we soon got tired of trying to top each other's big fish story, so we slept most of the way home. I'm sure that most of the gang, myself included has had good dreams about the Alaskan Fishing Smorgasbord - it truly was a fisherman's dream come true.

The End

Time to buy another of Bill T's books.

BOOKS WRITTEN BY
BILL R. THOMAS

	Title	Brief Description
1)	A Summer on Piney Creek	A Summer Spent with Friend Living in a Cave on Piney Creek (Kentucky)
2)	Hickory Fired Tobacco, Moonshine Whiskey, Beautiful Horses, and Fast Women	Kentucky Based Short Stories
3)	Bill T's Texas Bob Tales	Texas Based Short Stories
4)	I Smell Smoke	Authors Experience as B-47 Crew Member in Strategic Air Command
5)	My Most Memorable Adventures - One Hunting and One Fishing	Hunting Trip in Mexico and Fishing Trip in Alaska
6)	The Accumulated Wisdom of the Bugscuffle Domino, Whittle and Spit Club	Philosophy and Wisdom Gained Over a Colorful Lifetime
7)	The T-Bone Ranch	Developing a Cattle Ranch in Montague County, Texas
8)	A Wild Shot In The Dark	Autobiography - Birth Through Air Force
9)	The Debits Are On The Left, The Credits Are By The Window	Autobiography - Air Force to Present

www.ingramcontent.com/pod-product-compliance
Lightning Source LLC
LaVergne TN
LVHW011354080426
835511LV00005B/283

* 9 7 8 0 5 7 8 1 0 0 3 2 6 *